CUBA

One Moment in Time

Jackie Cannon

BALBOA.
PRESS
A DIVISION OF HAY HOUSE

Balboa Press books may be ordered through booksellers or by contacting:

Balboa Press
A Division of Hay House
1663 Liberty Drive
Bloomington, IN 47403
www.balboapress.com
1 (877) 407-4847

Print information available on the last page.

ISBN: 978-1-5043-5215-4 (sc)
ISBN: 978-1-5043-5217-8 (hc)
ISBN: 978-1-5043-5216-1 (e)

Library of Congress Control Number: 2016903835

Balboa Press rev. date: 04/14/2016

CONTENTS

FOREWORD

What do Raúl Castro, Barack Obama and a fridge have in common?

To most people, I am certain the answer is "nothing".

For me they came together in Havana's shopping mall at the junction of 3a and 70a, where my husband and I were on the lookout for a couple of domestic appliances. Specifically, we were negotiating the transport of a fridge we were about buy when we heard the news of somewhat more globally significant negotiations between the governments of Cuba and the U.S. This was the 17th December 2014, aka 17D.

We were to be in Havana for the next 2.5 months and here was an opportunity to experience history in the making.

I did not notice the amazing opportunity I had to record any of the experience in my own book until almost a month later when

I woke up one morning and told my husband about some vague half-dreamed conversation that had been happening in my head. There seemed to be so much new information, so many new conversations and so many puzzling (to me) interpretations that I found myself writing later that day in my own personal quest to make sense of the implications of what was happening.

That's why this book has been written.

It has only now arrived at the publication stage because I have lingered over my responses to every new event, spent hours back in fast internet territory scouring newspapers for updates, discussing how they fit with the Cuban mindset, how the Cuban people and government might respond, what benefits can develop for Cuba and the U.S., and what all of it means to me. That's how I have spent the last ten months since renewal of diplomatic relations were announced.

Despite my endless reading, discussing and absorption of facts, this book does not include them all. There is a relatively short chronology of what I consider to be the key events of 2015 at the end of the book, but this book is not merely about facts. Nor is this book designed for any specific group, whether tourists, potential investors, political activists, history buffs or any other specific group. It is not a history book. It is not a tourist guide. It is not a tale of cross-border love and obstacles. Nor is it designed as a cultural study.

That's what it is not. What it is, is a collection of moments. Moments which weave my experiences of Cuba into the historical, political and social tapestry as I have lived and perceived it. It is a series of snapshots of a moment in time, it reflects the short time before and the few months following the announcement of renewed diplomatic ties between the U.S. and Cuba after over 55 years of political stand-off between the governments of the two neighbouring countries, and my experiences in that context. It is also an overview of some of the conversations I have had with Cubans and non-Cubans, people who have visited the island and some who have not. Its focus is Cuba. I am not in a position to record views from every angle of the debate in the United States. For that, I have had to rely primarily on published sources available on the internet.

I make no claim that any of the scenarios are widely applicable, universally accepted or ever repeated. This is rather a series of snapshots of my experiences, an overview of some of my own observations, and a summary of my own perceptions and explanations that make sense to me. I trust your curiosity and interest will allow them to make sense to you too, provide valuable insights, enlighten your understanding of a process, and enrich your experience.

I make a plea to all who read this book to suspend all judgement. My mind has not been shaped according to the same circumstances that have shaped life in Cuba and the uniquely Cuban responses. Who am I to judge it? My job here is as a humble observer, recorder and student. I am delighted you are joining me in this exploration.

Like everything in life, the current situation in Cuba will change. My version of events is not exclusive nor conclusive, and there is information which I believe is important to record as the times, to paraphrase Bob Dylan, they are a'changin'.

You may find that some snippets reflect the romantic revolutionary visionary in me, inspired by Che Guevara's motorbike rides through peasant country before embarking on his unwavering journey with socialist/communist revolution as his destination. You will almost certainly identify that my mindset is shaped by Western capitalism.

ACKNOWLEDGEMENTS

I extend a profoundly heart-felt acknowledgement to my late father, James Cannon, and mother, Bridget (Cel) Cannon (née Leonard). Without their loving support, I would never have learned enough Spanish to have the career and experiences I have enjoyed, nor the funds and openness to travel. Mam and Dad, wherever you are, this is for you with love. And to my sister, Anne, you taught me a lot. This is a loving "thank you".

I have had many teachers. I have stood on the shoulders of giants. There is no order to the names included with huge gratitude: Uncle John; Teresa Lawlor; Barbara Phillips; Stuart Russell Cocks; Pat Odber; Berni Callanan; Sangita Patel; Par Kumaraswami; Toni Kapcia; Mayda Medina; Annie Grove-White; Rafael Pepiol; Kerry-Anne Mendoza.

To everyone who has made a financial contribution to the publication of this book - thank you. Especially to Mariabelle and Allan Headlam, Tim Law and Janice Pattison. Your belief in me has mattered more than the money.

Feedback and encouragement has also been received and appreciated from Paul Shepherd; Sarah Cullum; Cuban author José Ramón Torres; Lourdes Banegas and Carol Pool. All have extended a generous hand of friendship and support in ways that they already know, or maybe can't even imagine. Thank you for every conversation that has accompanied my steps.

Many many others have glittered my path to this stage, offering their time, their food and their shelter generously. Neil Price and Carrie Brookes – you stand out in this. Thank you for being the water-bearers on the rocky road.

The key acknowledgement has to go to my husband, José Arístides Rodríguez Chacón (Aris), without whose knowledge and nationality, and his willingness to share it with me, this book would never have been written. He's the one who has had to tolerate my questions, my impatience and my procrastination. He has also cooked, cleaned and repaired stuff while I sat in front of my computer reading to dissolve the mystery, and writing to share it with others. He has also had to sign endless reams of incomprehensible papers. Aris, thank you. I love and appreciate you!

Despite all the support I have had, the only person left to acknowledge is myself for sharing my experiences even though I know I will have misinterpreted stuff and got stuff wrong. Any and every error is exclusively attributable to me. Your feedback is welcomed. As a very good friend of mine has frequently said "It'll be all right in the end. If it's not all right, it's not the end."

Thank you for your interest in the start of this journey.

MOMENT ONE

Moments of a Meandering Mind

I am delighted you are joining me on this journey of curiosity. Thank you.

I have a few things to ask of you before we start this trip together.

First: that you let go of any ideas you may have about how a book should be structured and written.

Second: that you are willing to be my travel companion, open to observing and questioning and being simultaneously (or alternately) curious, amused, concerned, light-hearted, inquisitive, serious, fun-loving, and committed to playing a part in Cuba's evolution by learning or whatever peaceful way you find appropriate.

You will find I have depicted some moments more visually. Others report moments of reflection, more pensive interludes I have passed attempting to understand Cuba, its people, and their lives, the meaning of sovereignty, democracy, auto-determination, western media, overt and covert political agendas, anti-Cuban interests, pro-Cuban interests, alongside all sorts of other meanderings of the mind, and how all of this matters.

I have been especially interested in how Cubans so obviously have many difficulties to face while mostly appearing to deal with them with a self-effacing and positive attitude, commonly with an ability to throw in a comical spin on their society, their own social behaviours, difficulties, pleasures and circumstances.

Some of the scenarios outlined will be familiar to many tourists who have visited the island. Many others will paint a picture of certain realities that are familiar to Cubans both inside and outside the country, never even noticed by visitors. Others still will reflect my own curiosity and intimately personal experiences and bring life to small details that contribute to the whole, maybe never even noticed by Cubans.

Some of the information is drawn from external sources. It is information which has variously led me to think, be upset, disturbed, delighted, intrigued, or in some way or another led me to believe it is valuable to include here.

I offer no apologies for interspersing my own experience with what I have discovered from other sources. In many ways the randomness of what you will read, and particularly the order in which it is presented, is a true reflection of the haphazard way in which my experience has evolved. If you are willing to accept that, you may well enjoy the journey in the same way as I am.

MOMENT TWO

The Backdrop

The idea for this book surfaced one morning in January 2015. I completed it only at the end of October 2015. I find journeys don't always work out the way we plan them even though we get to the same destination in the end.

I and my *habanero* husband of three years and four months went back to see his family and start the process of setting up home. After a period working as a translator for the *Granma Internacional* newspaper, and, as a consequence of leaving the position, no longer having a place to live, we had bought a flat near the Miramar district of Havana in July 2013, funded out of having sold a house in Bristol (UK) after learning an unwanted lesson from some apparently trustworthy tenants (my mistake). On the up-side they taught me that maintaining a house with a mortgage on my imminent Cuban salary was unsustainable. (I'll tell you more about the Cuban salary bit later). Anyway, back in 2012 I learned that if all tenants had the same integrity levels as the beautiful family that moved in, I would end up having to give the house to the bank and lose any chance of equity. So I sold the house that I had temporarily let to the beautiful family. Those poor little girls, whose parents did what my dear old Dad would have called a "moonlight-flit" on me, apparently moved from one place to another promising to pay rent and cover utilities which never appeared!! Sometimes we get lessons we don't necessarily like but we can still get value from them. Anyway, recognising that my vocation was not as a landlady and being happy that they had gone, I was unwilling to throw away the chance of living and working in Cuba, so I sold the house. Off to Cuba with funds then available to supplement my salary and desired lifestyle.

After working in Havana for a relatively short while I was ready to return to the UK. The house sale had at least provided for the purchase of a modest apartment in Havana. So far so good. For a whole host of reasons, however, it was 17 months before we went back to see Havana, my husband's family and our new home. That was six days before the announcement of renewed diplomatic relations between Cuba and its powerful neighbours to the north.

MOMENT THREE

The Announcement

How I ended up in Havana in December 2014 is not a mystery. It is the result of a bunch of decisions I had taken in my life up to that time, some of which seem now to me more important than others. Others more or less intelligent. Some even risky and driven by emotion.

Much the same could be said of the political, social and economic context of relations between the U.S. and Cuba, which culminated in the announcements of Presidents Obama and Castro outlining their intention to resume diplomatic relations after so many years of tensions between the two nations.

Six days after our arrival, it seemed, happily in some ways, as if nothing would ever be the same again in Cuba. I, apparently like most of the rest of the world, had not expected this.

Working backwards in my life, certain elements combined to have it make sense for me to be in Havana for a couple of months at this stage in my life. I had been married for over three years to my husband, who was born and raised in Havana. He was one of the Cubans about whom so little is written, one of the invisible citizens so rarely talked about, who had travelled outside his homeland, and who had returned home. It seems, if one believes the stories of severe restrictions on the movement of Cubans, that most Cubans who travel outside their homeland are delighted to get away and not go back. My husband is one of many I now know who put paid to that myth. He, like lots of his Cuban friends who, for one reason or another, live abroad, loves his homeland.

He had travelled outside Cuba on one of his country's highly valued humanitarian missions. When we met in 2010, nevertheless, he was fully expecting to spend the next few years of his life, or maybe even the rest of it, doing what he could to ensure his octogenarian mother was comfortable and he was able to survive, before I came along and interrupted that. This (and he) has definitely been important for me and the writing of this book in terms of stimulating my interest in the country, and giving me the opportunity to extend and deepen my understanding of this so-long stigmatised archipelago of the Caribbean.

I considered myself to be somewhat of a learned specialist in Peninsular Spain. Having been a University lecturer in Spanish in the UK for almost 20 years, I expected to find some familiar aspects about Cuba. After all, it was a former colony, until 1898, of the Spanish Crown.

When I first went to Havana, I did find some elements which seemed familiar until I started noticing that I did not in fact understand what I was seeing. I was undeniably seeing it, but the opportunity and challenge was to attempt to gain an understanding of what I was seeing with a set of Cuban spectacles providing the filter, rather than through my own distortions and framework. My husband became my spectacles, my filter, as well as my guide, my instructor, my protector, and my personal shopper. He also became my work coach when he heard about a job he thought I might find of interest.

My interest in designing a life with my husband (we had married in August 2011) at a time when, as a technical specialist in the medical field, he still had to go through the extremely lengthy and burdensome administrative process of requesting permission to travel outside the country (one of the Cuban government's measures, since largely eradicated, to limit the potential – primarily U.S. incentivised – brain-drain after benefiting from a free university education in Cuba) provided me with an even greater opportunity. That's how come I ended up in the privileged position of working as a translator for the newspaper "Granma", an experience which provided an alarmingly sharp learning curve and plenty of opportunities for frustrations and friendships pretty much in equal measure.

What an opportunity, to work in Cuba and learn about a life there. And after 17 months away both I and my husband were keen to get back.

In December 2014, we were about to embark on a new phase. I was going to have an experience of my own home, with my own neighbours, family, friends and a TV to watch. It was about to be as close as any foreigner can reasonably get to living like a Cuban. And, I know you know it's not life as a real Cuban for a whole host of reasons.

I, like everybody else, can observe any number of things but I can only interpret what I see according to my own experience, perspective and knowledge. I have often watched fish in an aquarium, and however long I spend looking at them, watching them swim (in my view, usually aimlessly), darting towards the crumbs they are fed, flashing past each other, almost imperceptibly propelling themselves with their tails and their fins, I am clear I will never know what it is like to be a fish.

Somewhat bizarrely perhaps, I have found understanding Cuba, how it works and what has shaped the mentality of so many Cubans, to be akin to watching fish. I am not Cuban. I was not brought up in a country isolated from, stigmatised and even, one might argue, demonised by its closest neighbours and by so many other countries.

Many times I notice the way they behave or respond is understood by the Cubans while remaining a mystery to me even if I have some understanding and have benefited from some explanation. And I am not speaking about the language. I speak excellent Spanish. I have done for years. True, I have had to adapt to the local accent and ways of expressing day-to-day things, but my understanding has to go deeper than just the words. And that's a longer process.

MOMENT FOUR

A non-Cuban's understanding.
Is that an oxymoron?

I was born and raised in England, my cultural heritage is Irish Catholic, with all my grandparents coming from County Mayo in the Republic of Ireland, the heart of the most drastic depopulation of the 1840's famine through death and migration, an area where my mother was born and lived until the early years of World War II took her to nursing in the UK, and where my father spent every summer vacation. They carried inside them the many family inherited tales, often conveyed through melancholic musical ballads, of struggle and the search for a better life through the wrench of emigration. I guess that has given me a particular set of eyes which enable me to see and interpret what motivates people from a land of few opportunities to launch themselves into a world so often fuelled by racial and political hostility armed only with the phone number or address of some close or distant relative or neighbour and the simple human dream of reaching for a better life.

In that regard, I notice many similarities between Cuba and my own cultural roots. Both people are very family-oriented too. Similarities just about end there apart from how I choose to connect them and give my interpretations. My husband of course has his own personal interpretations and he has enlightened me on many occasions with details and overviews of Cuban living. This has so often occurred to me as just like the imperceptible propulsion of fins or the mindless darting about for crumbs. Many, like him, carry the memory of threatened survival after the collapse of the Soviet Union, when their main source of support dried up, a situation exploited by the U.S. to tighten the blockade in a so-far failed attempt to provoke regime change in Cuba irrespective of it being supported by up to 97% of the people on a 97% voter turnout in recent years, and disregarding the human damage that was being caused in the name of economic and political hegemony.

Little by little, I have been learning how to have a life that works in this country, what I need to sort out, who I need to contact, what I need to understand about the past to make sense of the present, and what is classed as appropriate behaviour. I have also been learning to leave many things to my husband, a challenge for an independent professional western woman, although it does ensure I don't clog the works of my life with my culturally incompetent flippers.

It is important to highlight that any inaccuracy, erroneous interpretation, omission in factual information, or ludicrous vision of reality is entirely mine. My husband does not read English so I cannot blame him for anything other than being Cuban, which is a bit like blaming the wind for blowing, despite the temptation to do so in my more challenged moments!

MOMENT FIVE

The Wedding Reception

Certain things that have happened in my life with my husband have led to hiccups in our communication due to my inability to understand what was shaping his behaviour, view or comments.

One early example was when, during my first visit to Havana, he did not want to come into the bar of the hotel where I was staying. I did not understand that his reluctance was borne out of the fact that Cubans for many years previously were not permitted to go into tourist hotels. That is no longer the case. I was the ignorant one for not being aware of it having been that way in the past. Fortunately I listened and learned as otherwise I could have made up an endless number of reasons why he did not want to join me for a drink in a hotel in the early days. No point boring you with my internal conversations – none of them now make sense.

The next memorable example was on our wedding day in August 2011. There was a tension between my husband and me stemming from my internal nattering and my lack of understanding and awareness. Failure to listen could have led to a very fast divorce. Here's what happened.

I had decided I wanted to celebrate with a few sundowners in the garden of the splendid *Hotel Nacional*, an event we were going to share with his mother, his two brothers, their partners, a small group of his friends and our witnesses. I hadn't invited anybody from back home to join me because I didn't want to have to play tourist guide while sorting out the necessary bureaucratic papers. I was happy to be embarking on this journey of married life in such a wonderful environment. And a liquid wedding breakfast for fourteen of us at the equivalent of 40USD per round struck me as a very affordable luxury. So we ordered a second round as the sun started its descent on the horizon. Two *mojitos* on my wedding day started calling for a third, just to extend the pleasure of the temperature, the vast expanse of sea in front of me, the breeze, the relaxation and the satisfaction of taking our next step in our now-joined future. Or maybe it was just because I felt a little bit tipsy as I teetered on the brink of a new uncharted life.

My suggestion to my husband for a third drink was met with a frown. He said some people were ready to leave. Let them! I retorted. Why should I limit my pleasure just because some other people want to do other things with their evening and join in the carnival that was happening on the Malecón below? It looked to me like I was having to act according to what others wanted rather than what I wanted.

It was a striking blow when I pushed my husband to express his real reason for wanting to wind up the party, and I actually listened. It was the moment I got in my gut how utterly ignorant I was and how insensitive it was of me to want to engage in such gross extravagance. He said "I'm just thinking of how much food my mum could buy with 40USD". Of course! The equivalent of two months' average salary for a Cuban. And I was proposing a THIRD round. Six months' salary on a few drinks! I realised right then how little I would enjoy a drink at a wedding in Europe with 14 attendees when each round of drinks was costing two months' salary. His family and friends were not used to the *Hotel Nacional*. Our guests did not know how low the cost seemed to me -only one of them had ever been outside Cuba- and it didn't look to me like the time to tell them. So we decided together that two drinks at sunset was plenty and it was now time to move to the next activity of the daily "*lucha*" (struggle), the way the Cubans so frequently refer to the daily grind or simply their activity *resolviendo*, solving the problems of life. Of course, nobody expected the newly-weds to spend the evening with them anyway so we were able to head off to our hotel and enjoy the included *Piña Coladas* by the pool.

Albert Einstein was right when he said the only source of knowledge is experience.

Curious snippet: Einstein visited Havana in 1930 and turned down the chance to stay at the *Hotel Nacional*.

MOMENT SIX

A New Approach

So back to December 2014.

We arrived in Havana on 11ᵗʰ December. We had given a few talks on Cuba while we were in the UK to different groups of people, and we returned to a Cuba pretty much as we had left it; a similar number of dilapidated buildings, people still busying themselves with their daily activities, and tourists doing what tourists do, some with greater knowledge and awareness than others of what they wanted to see and experience. Within a week the conversations had noticeably shifted. It felt like visitors and Cubans alike were aware they were witnessing history in the making.

In our own lives, we were venturing into a new phase. We were installing ourselves in the apartment we had bought in July 2013, but which had been left empty since then while we worked out some income in Europe.

Meanwhile, I, alongside many, had long had a belief that the U.S. Government sanctions and stance on Cuba would have to come to an end[1], particularly given that, in President Obama's own words "no other nation joins us in imposing these sanctions", but after over 55 years of punishing trade restrictions and unending hostilities, I wasn't holding my breath waiting for that moment to arrive. I certainly did not expect to hear from President Obama a week after we arrived that "these 50 years have shown that isolation has not worked, it's time for a new approach" (full reference included at the end of this book).

We didn't have a television for the first few weeks of being there so we didn't hear the news on the Cuban TV. How we found out about diplomatic relations being restored was not how I would have designed it, but then fact is often stranger than fiction.

As I mentioned previously, we were buying a fridge when we heard the news. Having come to our new and unfurnished flat we needed to put some basics in. So there were many reasons we were not listening to the news that week, amongst which was that we were in search of a few domestic appliances which did not cost the equivalent of several limbs (more about that later).

The first we heard of the announcements from the Presidents of the two countries was via a text message from an interested friend in the UK. The SMS which dropped into the phone around

---

[1] A valuable overview of U.S. Government hostilities by Richard A. Dello Buono in his chapter entitled "The Hostile Tides of Cuban-U.S. Relations" is offered in *Cuba in the 21st Century:Realities and Perspectives*, Editorial José Martí, 2005

3pm Cuban time, while we were negotiating the purchase of our much-needed fridge, read: "3 hours ago – Official – Obama seeks to resume full diplomatic ties with Cuba", followed five minutes later by "Cuba released Alan Gross today and the yanks [sic] released 3 Cubans insisting it wasn't a tit for tat!" I responded excitedly enquiring if the three Cubans released by the U.S. were the remaining three of the Cuban Five, and, knowing that the detention of the Cuban anti-terrorists is a topic unfamiliar to many British people, I asked for the names just in case he didn't know who the Cuban Five were. Such is the level of information received in the UK about Cuba that my pal did not know. He said the names had not been given. I doubted that was the case, it's just that he didn't know that the government and the people in the homeland were anxiously awaiting the return of their national heroes. I have no doubt more people know about the Cuban Five now, but maybe not. It has not been the main focus of the news outside Cuba.

In the month following the announcement by Presidents Castro and Obama, the conversation on the streets altered. There was a sense of anticipation, an opening of new opportunities, a certain excitement.

There was also a sense of pride. The then President of the Republic of Cuba and Historic Leader of the Revolution, Fidel (Castro) had promised back in 2001 that the five Cuban anti-terrorists would return home. After nearly 17 years since their detention, few would have been anticipating their release in 2014. And that day came, with President Obama describing as "outdated" the United States' policy towards Cuba, having "failed to advance [U.S.] interests". Some in the U.S. have undoubtedly been upset by this truth.

Associated breakthrough announcements were made on 17D. With immediate effect, U.S. tourists visiting Cuba could take $100-worth of alcohol and cigars, previously limited. A month later, on 15th January, President Obama announced new measures in commercial and tourist links with Cuba. People in both countries started talking about the news reports and the possibility of a U.S. Embassy in Havana and a Cuban Embassy in Washington, but everyone in Cuba was clear that full diplomatic relations would not happen until the U.S. Congress removed what the U.S. government calls the embargo and most in Cuba and many other places call the blockade, applied in the early years of revolutionary government and reinforced in successive laws culminating in the 1996 Helms-Burton Act[2]. The term *blobargo* has been used by some to capture the two terms according to perspective. Blockade and embargo.

---

[2] Documented in many sources but for context read *Cuba in Revolution: A History* since the Fifties, A. Kapcia, Reaktion Books, London 2008

MOMENT SEVEN

Frustration and friendship

It has sometimes surprised me that not everyone outside Cuba is aware of the conditions of the financial, commercial and economic blockade against Cuba. One friend wrote to me saying "Everybody's eyes are on Cuba now, with the lifting of the embargo." This sort of mis-construction of reality makes me sad (and frustrated) as it shows that people trust the mass media which is allowing so many to believe that what has happened between Cuba and the U.S. constitutes normalisation of relations. A few press sources report that a condition of normalisation is also the return of Guantánamo Bay. There's always the option to compensate or offer restitution for the damage and human suffering caused by the blockade but that is rarely highlighted, and is possibly a pipe-dream. The mis-information and dis-information leads people to know nothing while thinking they know something, and everyone goes away blissful in their own ignorance.

I refuse to stay ignorant and this leads me into quite a bit of upset at times but through this book, you will share part of the dawning moments of the last few years.

Some experiences I have had are odd. I did not plan them this way. And it didn't occur to me until months later to consider the reality of the impact of U.S. occupation of Guantánamo Bay. You might like to check this out yourself.

This was a visual experience I had not connected with until recently.

Go to a map of Cuba on google, say. Find Guantánamo in the south east. Zoom in further and check out the coast. There is a squared-off line marking the U.S. border. So what? Well, consider this... Cuba is an island. History shows that water provides good trading possibilities. So, how is it justifiable that, at a time when Cuba is attempting to develop its business potential using the Mariel port outside Havana, Guantánamo Bay, its largest natural port, 16 times the size of Mariel, is out of use for its own people because of U.S. occupation and yet President Obama is speaking of normalising relations without addressing the occupation while limiting Cuba's ability to make use of one of its major natural resources for the benefit of the people in the poorest province in the country? Didn't President Obama say he wanted to make life better for Cubans? Isn't it time the territory was returned to the sovereign republic? Or is normalisation only possible according to what the U.S. says is normal? Maybe we should take a look at the world to check out what can be classed as "normal".

Not all of my friends seem to be able to hear me.

MOMENT EIGHT

A Period of Rapid Change?

E leven weeks after the Presidential announcements, lifting the "embargo" was raised as an issue but not proffered by the U.S government as a necessary pre-condition to re-establishing diplomatic relations. At the time of updating this manuscript in October, the decision on whether or not to remove the blockade has still not been made. The blockade is still in place. As is the U.S. occupation of Guantánamo.

Certain key events have occurred. In April, Presidents Obama and Castro met face-to-face at the Summit of the Americas, a forum from which Cuba had been excluded for over 50 years. Cuba was removed from the United States' list of State Sponsors of Terrorism in May, their inclusion having no justification from the outset. Each country has opened an embassy on its neighbour's land, Cuba in Washington in July, the U.S in Havana in August.

Pope Francis visited Cuba in September and then flew direct to the U.S. on a pastoral tour.

The same week in September saw Raúl Castro speak at the United Nations, the first time he had addressed this body. The British newspaper *The Guardian*, reported (29 September 2015) that President Obama had said in his own speech to the UN earlier in the day:

> "I'm confident that our Congress will inevitably lift an embargo that should not be in place any more."

Even approaching President Obama's March 2016 visit, the embargo was still not lifted. And people can be left thinking that Cuba is holding things up, what with so many things, like buses, happening to such an intermittent timetable. It's also true that, despite the apparent forward steps to "normalising relations, the anti-Cuba lobby is still ensuring funds are available for the National Endowment for Democracy (NED), a fund used by the U.S. to undermine left-wing and socialist governments and support opposition groups by supposedly promoting "democracy." TeleSurTv[3] reported the following 13th June 2015:

> "The U.S. Committee on Appropriations approved on Friday US$30 million for "programs to promote democracy and strengthen civil society in Cuba, of which not less than US$8,000,000 shall be for NED," as quoted from the committee report.

In a context of alleged normalisation of relations between the two countries, it's mischievous to say the least.

---

[3] http://www.telesurtv.net/english/news/US-Allocates-Democracy-Funds-for-Cuba--20150613-0009.html

MOMENT NINE

Business Bonanza

New openings apparently now abound for businesses and an inflow of investment is anticipated, particularly taking advantage of, and kick-starting, the developing commercial port facilities and special trade zones already under construction in a number of Cuban ports. The main ones are Mariel outside Havana and also in Cienfuegos and Santiago de Cuba, but not Guantánamo.

Cuba will no longer be excluded from pertinent international organisations. Chinese investment partners and their representative specialists are already on the ground. Many more are set to follow.

Interestingly, this was clearly anticipated before December 2014 as Cuba had already passed its new foreign investment law in 2014 (law 188) as part of their ongoing economic updating programme.

I have learned that Mariel holds a very significant position in the minds of Cubans, although I was unaware of it back in 1980 when it happened, in a manner that now strikes me as somewhat ironic. It has always been a major port and it is logical that its natural depth should be supporting business interests with its capacity for larger maritime vessels, but I consider it worth a note that it was also the key location in 1980 for a boat-lift drama stimulated by the U.S and supported by the Cuban government, so the story goes. I will leave you to do your own investigation and reading on that subject, but knowing about it and its impact on the re-energising of revolutionary sentiment may well be crucial to understanding the Revolution's survival over more than half a century, a phenomenon outlined eruditely in various of Antoni Kapcia's and other experts' books on Cuba.

It was reported on the Cuban TV (*Mesa Redonda*, Cubavision channel, 2nd March 2015) that U.S. media are publishing on average 3 or 4 articles a day on Cuba. One can celebrate that the people of the United States, for so long provided with the image of a State sponsoring terrorism governed by a Communist dictator, are now receiving greater exposure to a different picture of Cuba. However, it was noted that even when the report is outlining and even exalting tourist facilities and the island's beaches, there always tends to be a comment on the politics of the island. You will notice that the same approach is not adopted in the west for the majority of tourist destinations.

MOMENT TEN

The Russian influence

One aspect of Cuba's current situation that merits a few comments is that the media tends to present the country as an abandoned outpost and relic of the Soviet bloc floating alone in the Caribbean. This is an interpretation of reality. It is not reality. Anything other than one's own experience cannot be classed as reality and I'm not even sure if that can be trusted.

That the Cuban archipelago is in the Caribbean, in fact, is only partially true since the Atlantic Ocean washes the north coast. Its closest point to North America is a mere 90 miles distance. Cuba's closest geographical neighbour, however, is a British territory, the paradise and safe haven of UK tax avoiders, the Cayman Islands.

Another angle of the image of the abandoned outpost is that, to me, it conveys an idea of something that was left to rot with the collapse of the Soviet bloc. While the fall of the Berlin Wall did signal a huge impact on Cuba and its people, the political stance of the Cuban Government was not adopted from Soviet communism. It was borne out of a post-colonial nation-building process and a stand for independence, national sovereignty and a right to self-determination, which had been subjugated to the U.S. empire.

The role of the former Soviet Union in Cuba's daily life can be perceived through many apparently random realities. One which I had not anticipated involved being in my friend Mayte's apartment and watching cartoons. In Russian! Many, maybe most, Cubans aged between 40 and 60 probably grew up with these programmes on TV and, as likely occurs with children everywhere, the images tend to stimulate fond memories of the carefree playtime of childhood. It seems it would be unrealistic to assert that many Cubans spoke Russian, but it is certainly true that many were exposed to the language on the radio and TV. But watching Russian cartoons probably influenced the children's political perceptions as much as Tom & Jerry did mine.

MOMENT ELEVEN

Making sense of the money

The whys and wherefores of the dual currency in Cuba are documented by many inside and outside Cuba. The Cuban Government is in the process of updating the economy and society with a number of measures introduced over the last few years, with others announced for the future. Merging or normalising the monetary system into a single currency is being discussed.

All I say for now, in case you did not know, is that there are two currencies in Cuba. There is the national currency (CUP – Cuban *pesos,* or *MN*) and there is the dollar-equivalent convertible currency (CUC). Cuban pesos can only be exchanged legally against CUCs at an exchange rate in official exchange bureaux of 25 pesos to the CUC. All foreign currency is converted into CUC so this is what most tourists have, unless they have exchanged some of their CUCs into MN inside Cuba.

It is a controversial system which I am not about to exalt or condemn. Nor explain.

It is the source of a whole host of anomalies, including income imbalances, differentiated levels of choice of where to shop, qualified professionals working in unqualified roles, such as taxi driver doctors, and theft.

There is very little street crime in Cuba, with crimes against foreign tourists subject to heavier penalties than those committed against Cubans (a measure intended to protect tourists in a country so dependent on the hard currency derived from their visits). It seems almost accepted that in a country of such scarcity most of the theft should be from public institutions and sold by the neighbour after the odd buck has been added for the middlemen. Small-scale pilfering offers, for many, a way of increasing one's income in a small way. With so much small-scale theft within public institutions, one could define it as large-scale. Suffice to say that theft from public organisations has been identified by President Castro as an issue to be addressed and eliminated.

When I worked in the newspaper, I, like my colleagues, received a monthly income of 415 pesos (MN), equivalent to a meagre 16USD. In addition, I received a stipend as a foreign specialist worker recognised by the State as contributing to Cuba, so, as well as being provided with living accommodation, I received a further 120USD equivalent per month. I was, as a result, comparatively wealthy. That said, it was not enough for me to live the kind of life I wanted and hoped for in Cuba. I liked having a beer by the water and they were a dollar each.

One aspect that I have found particularly challenging in Cuba is overcoming my western mindset. Particularly in terms of wanting to go out for dinner occasionally or have a few drinks in a nice location. There are plenty of nice places serving delicious food in Havana and it all seems cheap to me when I get distracted from reality and calculate the prices in pounds sterling. When I remember that my main income is in Cuban pesos everything rises sharply in price.

Many working in the tourist industry can be classed as relatively wealthy in this society as a few tips in dollars makes a huge difference to income. We foreigners bringing our own hard currency savings into Cuba can afford to top up the basics with a few luxuries like olive oil. My tastes are rather expensive.

Prices of many items are very high, although the basics of life are cheap in Cuba, if one has the time to go to the fresh food markets and buy direct from the producers, eking out an existence on the "*canasta básica*", literally the basic basket, provided as a subsidised social benefit to all Cubans through the "*libreta*", so often mistakenly referred to (outside Cuba) as the ration book when, rather than rationing consumer supply, actually ensures a minimum of rice, chicken, eggs, beans, sugar, coffee and cooking oil to each citizen.

However, from my own experience and from what many people in Cuba have told me, what is provided is simply not enough to sustain life. Nor is it what they used to receive before the "Special Period (in time of peace)", a series of cutbacks and measures introduced in response to the disappearance of most foreign supplies after the collapse of the Socialist bloc. Prior to 1989, the basic basket included a much wider range of essentials including soap, washing detergent and even shaving razors, now only available for purchase. These can be bought in the MN shops when they are available, which is not always, meaning they may have to be bought in the dollar stores.

The currency anomaly is even greater when it comes to buying imported items, particularly white goods. Except for when the Government announces a subsidised exchange programme, such as they did for refrigerators in recent years, such essentials have to be bought in convertible currency. As the self-employed sector grows, encouraged by recent Government policy, so there are more Cubans who, maybe through opening a restaurant, or a photography service, have access to tourist "dollars". The still large sector of public workers get paid in Cuban pesos, many of them never even having become familiar with the denominations of coins and notes in CUCs.

My own husband was initially as lost with CUCs in his own country as he was with pounds sterling when he first visited England. It reminded me of hours spent as a child playing "Monopoly", always wanting to win but knowing that I was using only play notes. I realised I was more familiar with the CUC notes as a tourist than my husband was as a Cuban. It was challenging to my mind, but understandable as he had lived like many, and maybe most, Cubans, being paid in MN and somehow making it last the month taking into account the income of the other working adults in the house. I haven't had to do it but I know it's hard to live on that amount of money, even in Cuba. It is one of the reasons I believe most foreign visitors will never understand what they are seeing as their foreign currency will always allow them more advantages than Cubans currently enjoy.

My husband's 2-year old god-daughter, on the other hand, has grasped the distinction of the currencies. This little one received a gift of 2 dollars from a family member who was working overseas. She squirrelled them away and the next time she went to get the coins out she found her mother had swapped them for 2 Cuban pesos in *moneda nacional*. The scandal was heard along the street as the toddler remonstrated with her mother demanding her "peshos".

MOMENT TWELVE

The price of utilities

When we were living in my *Granma*-provided apartment, I was not responsible for the utility bills. That was all included in what was provided for me as a "*medio básico*", the term to describe accommodation provided by the State to designated people, of which I had become one as a foreign specialist, a "*Técnica extranjera*". As a consequence, I never had to enquire into how much the bills cost.

Living now in our own apartment, I have discovered how ridiculously cheap (to my mind) certain utilities are, and how impossibly expensive many other items are.

My husband went along to the local water company to change the bills into his name and came back with some very surprising news. The water supply to our flat is unmetered so we pay a monthly

30

rate. And that rate is one (yes, one) *peso cubano* (MN), equating to about 2.5 pence per month (£0.025), or 4cents (USD).

The electricity bill came in at just over $2USD for one month, albeit without using the air-conditioning. The gas bill has yet to be determined. And I expect it to be even cheaper, especially compared to the bank-breaking amounts to be paid in the UK or Spain (or many other countries, I suspect).

In fact, when I attempted to rent out my house in the UK, I landed myself a problem as the unscrupulous liars never paid a penny in rent and left me with their electricity, gas and water bills. They taught me a great lesson, though.... That I could not afford to cover the associated costs on a Cuban salary if I could not guarantee income. No standing charges in Cuba. What a relief.

The phone is another matter. Landline to landline calls within the same municipality are staggeringly cheap. We don't currently have a phone at home and we have been told that there are no further lines available in our neighbourhood. But, I have been informed by several people that, as with many things in Cuba, a line could be available if we were willing to pay for it. It would only cost us about 800CUC. That's not a typo. That's eight hundred dollars! And people have said it like it's got to be worth it. I have been told that, as a foreigner, with a right to residence here, I could request a phone line and internet and miraculously the deficit of further lines disappears and one shows up to be subsequently charged in CUC. I recognise the need for hard currency, but I am currently unwilling to provide so much of it for what is not an essential requirement of mine right now.

So why would I not be tempted to install a phone in the house right now, despite it being very useful for my husband to make contact with his family and friends? We don't want to spend that amount of money on a phone when I (the one who most uses the phone in Europe) have so few people to call in Cuba, when either of us can call from a public phone or make a quick mobile to mobile call or text them, or when we can even go and visit. Apart from the fact I would rather direct that money towards something like a spare bed or maybe some comfortable chairs, there would be two main reasons that I would not want to shell out that money for so little return.

The first is that a phone line will not give me automatic access to internet. That has to be requested separately. Telecommunications are underdeveloped, as you might expect. The second is that if I was wanting friends back in the UK to call me in Cuba, I think I would have to pay for the calls in advance myself. Phone calls from the UK to Cuba are, in my opinion, eye-wateringly expensive. I have no idea if the cost is a result of the punitive Helms-Burton Act, aimed at criminalising the business relationships of third countries trading with Cuba, so any phone operator may pay a penalty for offering phone services to Cuba. It may be that or it may be because the U.S. blockade has resulted in limited access to bilateral agreements with ETECSA, Cuba's national telephone company. Or it may be because the Cuban Government has restricted access to telephone, communication and broadcasting facilities to ensure the likes of Radio Martí, overtly propagandist broadcasts from the anti-Cuba lobby in the U.S designed to undermine and destabilise Cuba's political regime, don't get transmitted. Or it could be a combination of all of these things. Or a simple lack of infrastructure maintenance and development. I could only guess.

What I don't have to guess is that when I first started calling Cuba in 2010, my usual phone operator in the UK quoted me £1.76

(over $2.5) per minute. After searching the internet I came up with a company called Rebtel, which was charging 64p/minute (approx $1/m) at the time. It has since gone down to around 55p, with discounts for buying a monthly or weekly package, reducing the cost to around 28p/m at the cheapest rate to Cuban mobiles or landlines, on top of which one pays 15% tax.

I was unsurprised when I heard that one of the first commercial areas that the U.S. is looking to develop in the Cuban market is telecommunications. I have to say that if that enables me to access VOIP services, have internet at home, and make calls at an acceptable cost, I will be delighted and my life will be further enhanced there. It would make permanent emigration far more attractive for me.

Nevertheless, my welcoming attitude to the telecommunications news was muted. I found it curious to note that the announcement of renewed diplomatic ties with Cuba came at the same time as an exchange of prisoners. The U.S. released the remaining 3 detainees of the Cuban Five while the Cuban Government released Alan Gross, a U.S. citizen detained on the island for allegedly engaging in the unauthorised distribution of telecommunications equipment. The U.S. interest in installing telecommunications on the island has been mentioned many times this year.

MOMENT THIRTEEN

Lost in translation

One of the elements that motivated me to write a personal record of observations and interpretations is that it provides you, the reader, with a series of anecdotes which are based on real experience, events which I have attempted to understand from my own and from a Cuban perspective and from which I have drawn my own conclusions. I do not demand you believe any of what I say, particularly with my own process of reaching conclusions. I continue to invite you to discern, do your own observation and research, and draw your own conclusions. I particularly invite you to visit Cuba as nothing is an adequate substitute for personal experience.

To me, this is key as I learned many years ago that it is important to be discerning when one reads anything, whether in a newspaper, a book or on the internet. I and most of my peers and subsequent generations, I would assert, have not been well trained in evaluating the information we receive.

So here comes a very personal view of mine... What we call our State education system in the UK (and, I guess, many other parts of the western developed world) is primarily geared to inputting (into the minds of youngsters) information in order for it to be output at some examination stage with a view to determining whether a student is smart enough to progress to university or not, or to define his/her professional possibilities. My understanding is that the etymology of the word "education" comes from the Latin "ex ducare", roughly meaning "to lead out from", in other words, "to bring out the best of what people already have within them". Personally I prefer this approach to education as it enables students to define their own needs and interests, and for me it is broader than an 11-year preparation for developing further study for work skills, or simply work skills for those not interested in entering Higher Education.

I could point to certain aspects of the Cuban education system, internationally heralded for its health education and literacy programmes which were extended across the country and abroad in the early years of the Revolution, but that is not my intention here.

What is important to me is that people are able to discern reality from non-reality. I had a couple of excellent, inspiring lecturers when I was an undergraduate years back. They know they inspired me and I am eternally grateful to them as without them I would not have had the life I have enjoyed so far, with my experience in Spanish-speaking countries having such a character-shaping impact on who I have become, that work in progress that I call me.

Why their contribution was so important to me has many facets but one of them was their own personal interest in keeping themselves up-to-date with what was happening in Spain in the last years of Spain's Francoist regime through the early years of the so-called transition to democracy.

One of the moments which marked me was in 1981 when one of them returned from a visit to Spain, abandoned the class she had previously outlined, and gave us copies of a range of newspapers from the day after 23-F, the day of the attempted coup when a certain military man named Tejero entered Parliament and ordered all the representatives in the house to the floor in an attempt at overthrowing the government, eventually frustrated. The newspapers included the recently established post-Franco "El País", and the right-wing "ABC". I can't remember the others but what did stay with me was that I read a very varied set of reports about what had happened, ranging from a generally impartial account of the facts to the right-wing press referring to Tejero, the leader of the assault on the democratically elected Parliament, as "el caballero" (the gentleman). The benefit of that experience has been applied to several decades of my reading and listening to news reports from many countries and a multitude of sources on a whole host of subjects.

My interest in learning about Cuba has undoubtedly been influenced by that learning experience. Happily, for many years I have had unlimited access to an ever-increasing number of sources in books, the press and particularly on the internet. I have seen many times how one event is recounted in many different ways. I have to assume this is as a result of the intention of the author to highlight whatever it is s/he thinks is the most valuable. The intention of a translator is also important for transmitting whatever is deemed to be the most appropriate version of a report.

I knew this way before working on the Cuban newspaper and it was always clear to me before I arrived that whatever was written would have to be in line with the overall political intention of the editorial board.

I believe this is always the case with any published or broadcast material. And most newspapers are able to employ or contract the people who are able to reflect the political intention of the publisher or broadcaster in their translations.

But why does that matter?

Well, it seems to me that one has to take particular care when reading or hearing anything about Cuba. As you know, salaries in Cuba are very low. That makes it difficult for Cuban publishing houses to have a band of translators able to respond with a fast turn-around time to news events. It also means many articles never get translated. Most academics who may have important scientific breakthroughs to share, do not have access to international journals as they do not have the money to pay specialised translators or editors. There are, of course, some translators in Cuba who do a good job of transmitting foreign language versions of news. Other than these, there are many bilingual English-Spanish speakers, perhaps mainly in Miami and the U.S. territories closest to Cuba. In other words in the traditional hotbed of the anti-Cuba lobby.

I assert that these elements contribute to a problem with any information about Cuba which is not translated by impartial specialists. I am not saying all translations are anti-Cuba, nor should they be pro-Cuba, but I am saying that the absence of balance makes it difficult to discern the most accurate reports of events in or relating to Cuba unless you are able to understand the original texts in Spanish. The almost indiscriminate use of Socialism/Communism in many texts is one example of this.

To give you an idea of what type of imbalance I am referring to here, I recently read about Cubans who had travelled temporarily, or maybe left Cuba permanently. What I did notice however is that the particular article referred to these people as "escapees". This was probably not translated and it is certainly unlikely to have been written by a pro-Cuban, and is clearly not impartial. Maybe it's just because I have a major interest in words and the use of language but it seems to me that unless one is alert when reading such texts, we find that we almost unconsciously adopt an interpretation (certainly no accident) which leaves us with a sense that Cubans are prisoners in their own country. Who else needs to escape, if not a prisoner?

My mother went to work in England to train as a nurse and expand her opportunities. I guess that could be called escaping poverty, although I never remember that term being used. I went to work in Spain and I have no recollection of anyone ever alleging that I escaped from the UK just because I wanted to develop my skills and opportunities in another country. So what makes temporary or permanent emigrants from Cuba so different?

Of course there are those from around the planet who have had to escape from their homeland and claim political asylum in another country. And there are Cubans who have done this, and some have used it as a handy excuse for gaining permanent resident status in some countries. And there is the "Cuban Adjustment Act" in the U.S. which, under their "wet feet, dry feet" policy, one could conclude had almost encouraged such migration as another way of working towards successive U.S. governments' objective of undermining Cuban sovereignty and the country's political regime.

I know some Cubans who are married to foreigners who live in Cuba, and some who have chosen to develop their lives and loves in other countries, temporarily if not permanently. I also am aware of some people wanting to "escape" to look forward to a life of materialism and multiple TV channels. I wish them well.

What I am clear about is that many Cubans would welcome the right to travel with the same conditions as we enjoy in the so-called developed west, although as far as I am aware, far from the majority would class that as escape, simply an exercise of their freedom to travel. Limitations to the exercise of that freedom are generally imposed via sometimes apparently random visa requirements by the countries they hope to visit rather than the one they are leaving.

MOMENT FOURTEEN

Cuban "escapees"

The text I read which referred to Cubans who had travelled abroad to live or work as "escapees" triggered a reaction of irritation bordering on anger in me as I am clear that Cuba is not a prison. So why would one ever need to escape when one is not detained?

Part of the reason why we were in Cuba for three months is specifically because my husband would have been as happy to stay in his own country, particularly on account of his family and the comfort of what is familiar. We chose to marry. I love many elements of life in Cuba while at the same time finding certain aspects extremely challenging and inconsistent with the way I want to live, primarily in terms of the access to the sort of income that will cover the cost of intercontinental travel, and the limitations of finding opportunities and generating such an income supported with easy internet access.

In Spain and the UK many people have sympathised with me on some of the administrative difficulties of having married a Cuban. Years of misinterpretation of a particular set of travel restrictions imposed by the Cuban Government have understandably left many people abroad believing that Cubans cannot leave Cuba. That is neither an absolute nor a legal truth and my conversations with Cubans in which many have told me about their travels confirm to me that it never was actually the case that Cubans could not travel. That said, there were restrictions. Add to those the fact that most have never had the financial resources to go anywhere. If they are invited by a friend or family member overseas, they have to face the administrative and visa obstacles and restrictions of host countries. It was not the case, however, that they were not permitted to leave Cuba, although they did have to return a minimum of once every 12 months (now two years) in order to ensure they retained rights to their assets in Cuba.

I have met a number of Cubans in Cuba who studied overseas, particularly in the former Soviet bloc. This can be understood in a political context of Cold War US/USSR hostilities.

I have met a larger number of Cubans who have participated in the type of humanitarian mission which resulted in more Cuban medics in Haiti after the earthquake than the totality of medics from all other countries. Similarly, more recently in Sierra Leone in the fight against Ebola, or the devastating earthquake in Nepal.

I have met several academic colleagues from Cuba who have visited other countries to participate in conferences or take up academic posts for a number of years.

Then there are the many Cubans who have travelled to the U.S. or Europe invited by family members, or friends.

I have met all these people in Cuba because they did not "escape". They returned home, just as I do after I go on holiday, attend a conference, or work in another country for a period of time. This might be called "circular migration". It does not much matter what we call it, only that we recognise that, despite the nonsense that is often presented in the media, it looks to me like most Cubans prefer to be at home.

Of course there are cases of Cubans who have violated their visas and remained illegally in another country or claimed asylum. A random episode I recall was of meeting a Cuban at one of the London airports who was looking for the right terminal to catch his connecting flight. As often happens with people of the same nationality in far-flung foreign places, he heard us talking and latched onto my husband's accent and a conversation ensued. He told us how he was heading back to Cuba to see his "esposa" (how Cuban men often refer to their partner even if they are not formally married) and child, who he hadn't seen for around eight months. He also told us how he had somehow arrived in some part of the European Union (I simply can't remember where or how that had happened), he claimed asylum and in order to remain in a specific country, he paid a woman to marry him so as he would have the right to residence. And he was doing what so many people do in other parts of the world, spending several months with his family, and then spending the remainder of the year working away to ensure the family has whatever it is decided the family needs. I guess he would count statistically as an "escapee", but it seemed to me from the conversation that he considered Cuba his home and he was just doing what worked for his life and income aspirations.

So we find most Cubans were allowed to travel. And many didn't. And there are other reasons.

Cubans who are employed have had to get a letter of authority from their employer to release them for up to six months to be submitted with visa applications. As far as I know, that is still the case.

Another aspect of the "escapee" topic has occurred to me. I have noticed that Cubans sometimes use the adjective "escapado/a". It appears to mean "great" or "in a class of (his/her) own". I have only ever heard that word used in Spain to mean "escaped" and I have been wondering of late if this is a throwback to the days of slavery. It's just an idea. I have no evidence to support my mind's meanderings.

MOMENT FIFTEEN

Siege mentality

I also wonder if the word "escape" might be used on account of feeling trapped or under siege. I have wondered about this one over a few years now. Through my reading of various articles and texts on Cuba, I have begun to understand what a siege might feel like. Cuba has, after all, been subjected to a blockade for over 50 years and although President Obama has used his executive powers to renew diplomatic relations, a decision on ending the blockade has yet to be taken by Congressional vote.

Three or so years ago I read what I found to be a very interesting book by Stephen Smith, a UK journalist, called *Cuba: The Land of Miracles*. There was a section in that book that brought up a concern for me. It was basically suggested that many or most Cubans would be willing to take up arms to defend their country. Being a pacifist, I thought it a good idea to check this out, as it worried me. I don't feel any particular loyalty to any country, a country, in my view, being an entity invented by man to ensure his own survival or dominate his neighbour. I don't align myself to a particular country. I have a right to nationality in two countries. Which one is my country? What if they decided to go to war with each other? Which should I defend? So, my personal stand is that a country is some land on this planet that was here before I arrived and will still be here when I leave this mortal plane so, much like the Native American Indians, I belong to the Earth, the Earth cannot belong to me. But that is just my personal stand and I recognise it does not fit with the current system of hegemony and planetary organisation.

So back to my concern. I, undoubtedly like many other visitors, have noticed a shipping container on Galiano Street in central Havana, set up as a rifle practice site. I have never seen anyone using it but I have seen the small step in front which, like at the fairground, allows the little people to get a good view for taking aim. As this is not a commercial activity, I have concluded that it is an opportunity for the people to continue to hone their shooting skills in case of attack. Maybe the threat of a competent volunteer revolutionary army is just what is needed to avoid attack.

So what was the result of my straw poll on whether Cubans would take up arms?

I asked a few friends, male and female, if they would defend their country and, without exception, they said they would. I have no evidence to demonstrate that many Cubans are trained in the use of arms but it appears that their pride in their country has provided a great enough defence to stave off further large-scale attacks from their neighbours in the north. Being under fear of attack brings out a need to defend in humans anywhere, I guess.

MOMENT SIXTEEN

Food Shopping in Havana

On many streets across Havana, you can see carts piled with fruit and veg. They sell in CUP/MN, at a rate which tends to be a bit above the prices you get in the market. It's hard to tell how much more because when they see the foreigner approach, it seems their scales become instantly laden before any purchase goes on them or the prices suddenly rise, but then that is just one of the consequences of being a foreigner in a country of scarcity. They don't know I live here on a Cuban income with no remittances from abroad, with a husband who has not been able to work on his various visits to me in the UK over the last few years.

The flower lady who cycles past our house every day has never overcharged me though. I bought 5 tiger lilies (a total of 20 Cuban pesos, 80c in USD) and 3 beautifully scented stock flowers at 3 pesos a stalk, all on the verge of bursting into bloom. The whole lot cost 29 Cuban pesos, just over a dollar. I gave the lady 30 pesos and asked if one of her flowers was for sale at 1 peso. She didn't have the change so she gave me another stem of stock. I bought from her again and overpaid on one occasion to compensate for my earlier cheekiness. The flowers were totally fresh and lasted over a week, with a delightful aroma as the evening closes in, bringing nature into our living room.

You will also generally find someone in markets selling plastic bags at a peso each. There are other street vendors (voceadores) who announce their wares as they pass. I can't understand most of what they say but my husband deciphered the vocal advertising from the guy who was offered mattress repairs *in situ*.

The equivalent of the ice cream van has been round a few times, usually a bicycle towing a refrigerated box. Curiously, the jingle is recognisable as an ice-cream van even though the tunes have included "Silent Night", "Jingle Bells", and "London Bridge Is Falling Down". In early February, I heard "Oh, come all ye faithful" and "Hark the herald angels sing". I suspect Cubans have no idea of what they are hearing. My husband didn't know, but these jingles shift my perspective of time and place, being more accustomed to hearing them around Christmastime with the threat (or promise, depending on your attitude) of snow, back in the UK.

Then there is the old guy strolling down the street with a Tupperware container selling "coquitos", a sugar and coconut sweet, announcing what is obviously a home-made product. We didn't try them but my mother-in-law made some sweet coconut paste which was delicious on cheese. Note to self... find out the recipe.

Similar to the ice-cream jingle in the sense that you have to recognise what you are hearing, every day there is a guy who passes on a bike with a kind of whistle. It was clear to me that he was offering some kind of product or service but of course I had to ask what it was as I never saw the guy and never heard him yell about anything. It turns out that he offers a knife- and scissor-sharpening service and his whistle lets you know he is in the area. All good as long as you know what you are hearing.

We also had a guy come to the door selling insecticide. Happily my husband was home and was able to get the instructions for use, so he has been able to apply that to any dank corners he has found, and although we had not seen many, we have been able to finish off the few cockroaches who had made the dark humid nooks and crannies their shelter in the time the flat had been closed up. I have since learned that these vendors are not self-employed salesmen but part of a brigade coordinated by the local clinic to offer preventative and anti-infection projects. The insecticide they have devised certainly does what it says on the tin. I never saw a live cockroach in our apartment.

All of these salesmen offer very Cuban products at Cuban prices. There are others who sell all sorts of other items, largely food like smoked salmon, tuna or chicken, on the black market in CUCs. The difference between them seems to relate to the source of the item for sale. But sometimes maybe it is just better not to know.

MOMENT SEVENTEEN

Plastic bags

If you want to buy in the market and the places where Cubans shop, including for bread, you will very quickly learn the importance of having a supply of clean and practical plastic bags tucked away in a pocket or whatever purse you have with you.

Most of the shops selling in CUCs have plastic bags in which they pack your purchases for free. It hasn't happened to me for a long time, but I have known even some of these CUC shops to run out of bags.

It was during my first visit to Cuba that I came across the word "jaba" (bag). The value of me using the word became clear almost immediately. Apart from the fact it lets the sellers know that while I may as well have "foreigner" plastered across my forehead, I DO have some considerable familiarity with Cuba. I had never come across the word in Spain.

I let myself down one day by heading out for bread without a bag. Fortunately the local bread shop is opposite the market and there was an old chap selling at the standard local price - a peso per bag. Sometimes I forget what is needed to just go and get the daily freshly-baked bread, usually costing 3pesos per stick loaf (about 7.5p). One day I was clearly not thinking straight when I went out with no Cuban pesos and there was no point going home to get some as my husband was out and I knew I didn't have a stash at home. This ended up meaning that I had to buy at the neighbouring shop in CUCs, costing around four times as much.

Partly because of the fact that anything I buy with Cuban pesos tends to cost more than my husband pays on account of my being seen as a foreigner, and by implication, naturally wealthy (ahem!), I tend to just keep a few Cuban peso notes in my purse particularly for any ride into town in a *botero* or a *taxi rutero* (more on that later). I don't bother with coins usually. Anything that requires coins, like the bus or the fruit and veg market is best reserved for my husband, or at least for when I am with him.

One day I caused a laugh of familiarity when I bought some AAA batteries at a shop in the Business Centre in Miramar. Given the location, I was paying in CUCs. The attendant was about to put a dual AAA battery pack in a bag and I laughed saying I didn't need the bag for the batteries but I would take it anyway as it would always come in handy. The old familiar scarcity conversation. If you're offered something in Cuba, you take it, whether or not you need it. If you don't need it, then someone you know will and you will be able to hand it on or maybe even sell it. I personally would not bother selling a *jaba* but there are other items which could be of value.

MOMENT EIGHTEEN

Getting around Havana

There are various options.

You might walk, drive your own or a hired car, catch a bus, hop on the city tour bus, take a private taxi, use one of the multi-passenger minibuses (*taxi rutero*) or one of the old American cars operating a passenger service, known as "*boteros*".

I'll make a comment on each option in its own mini-section as there is plenty to say on each, even though most tourists wouldn't have experienced some of them, many not even wanting such experiences. Transport in Cuba has provided every emotion for me from frustration en route to bewilderment, passing through amusement on the way.

I would point out that until you are confident with Spanish and understanding the way Cubans speak, some of these travel options may not be the most practical for you as they may require negotiation, best sorted before you actually get in, for example, a taxi unless it is one of the State taxis with a meter, which will definitely be one of the most expensive options. The other most expensive option is allowing a taxi driver to charge what he likes because you didn't negotiate the price beforehand – and it may well still seem quite cheap to you with your foreign currency and notion of taxi prices back home.

On the other hand, if the rains come, you might, like many *habaneros*, decide to stay put or at least seek shelter until it stops!

I am a large lady and some of what I say here may be influenced by that condition.

Nevertheless, some things are worth highlighting.

<u>Walking in Havana</u>

There are many old and dilapidated buildings. Where they exist, it is usually the best option to walk under the portals rather than on the pavement. A key hazard, due to the state of decay of some of the balconies, is that of falling masonry. Another is the risk of overflowing water pipes as people fill the roof-top water tanks. It is not unknown for people to throw water or even rubbish out of their windows. All of this adds to my personal preference to walk under the portals wherever possible.

That said, as well as looking up at the potential risks above, you need to keep a keen eye on the ground. Some might find a charm in the state of disrepair of much of the city. It can certainly help to understand Cuba's progress as it's an undeniable consequence of years of focus on politics, the defence of the homeland and the siege mentality, with economic updating, and tarting up the city centre, having become a priority much more recently.

Underfoot, there are many holes, cracks in the pavement, trees pushing up pavement slabs causing uneven surfaces, manholes with and without the appropriate covers, and various metal plates serving ventilation shafts and other functions. Many of them are rusty and you see people avoiding treading on them. I follow their footsteps, i.e. I go round the edges, because, to quote the comedian Steve Hughes "my parents taught me not to be a moron".

You may notice as well that Cubans do not generally step in water in the street, even if it is clear that it is just draining from someone's front porch that they have just washed. Of course, after heavy rain the drainage system can struggle and stagnant water is the ideal environment for all sorts of bugs and bacteria to thrive so they tend to ensure they are not forced to step in that either. Happily, after heavy rain, what has not drained away tends to evaporate quite quickly, so it is usually only a temporary problem.

Driving

Buying your own car is very expensive in Cuba, prohibitively so for many. If you are working for a private company, you may be able to buy a car as a foreign specialist worker (*técnico extranjero*). Car buying is not an area I have experience in and the rules have changed and may change again in this regard, so you would have to take professional advice on the current state of play for that one.

As someone used to being able to get a good car hire deal via travelsupermarket.com or some such comparison site, I have found hiring a car in Cuba is beyond my budget at around $70 per day. It's an option probably best reserved for travelling around the country, rather than being based in or near the city. As a result, I have not had the opportunity to do anything other than observe driving in Cuba, round the city and out on the open road. It appears to be a good idea to know where the horn controls are. It also appears to be useful to have 360 degree vision without moving your head as hazards can come at you from any angle.

Local buses

These offer the cheapest option. You need to find out what routes they operate on as the route is never displayed at the bus stop. Even the existence of a bus stop is often not clearly displayed. Or maybe I have just not learned to identify them well.

Local buses cost 40cents of a Cuban peso. With a Cuban peso at current exchange rates equating to just over 2.5p, the bus fare costs just about one penny. And that is irrespective of however far you travel.

At certain times of the day and on certain routes, buses can get very crowded, and that means crowded beyond what would legally be permitted under Health & Safety legislation in the UK that allows only a limited standing capacity. Buses are the standard form of transport for the majority of Cubans. Some other forms of transport may seem cheap to us but my 88 year old mother-in-law's 200-peso pension means she refuses to get a cab 20 blocks along the road to her son's house. That would cost 10 Cuban pesos, so a multi-cab would eat a big chuck of dough and she, like many Cubans I have met, is very proud and stoically willing to make do with what she has.

There are several aspects to catching a bus that I have not yet understood. One is that even where there is a bus stop, sometimes buses stop short or overrun the stop. This causes the fit ones to break into a canter or a gallop to jump on. Drivers rarely open the back doors to allow people to alight at the same time as they allow people to board, presumably so as to avoid people boarding without paying. And doorways get pretty jammed. One day I saw a guy get off the bus near the shopping mall at the junction of 41 and 42 Street in Playa. He stepped down via the back door clumsily dragging his shopping trolley full of bags of savoury biscuits. The bus was crammed with people on a Friday lunchtime and I cannot imagine he wheeled his trolley through the bus from the front doors past fellow passengers. It is certainly not uncommon for a bus to resume its route with the doors still open and people clutching the rails. I'll take a guess that this is to do with never knowing when the next bus will turn up so you are kind of best advised to jump on when yours passes, however jam packed it is.

You can still occasionally spot a double-humped "camello", literally "camel", introduced by the Cuban government in the fuel-starved 1990s. These were buses designed to carry yet more passengers to economise on fuel usage with the collapse of their main oil supplier, the Soviet Union. Some of these can still be seen around the city but they are not the most usual run on the bus routes.

My husband gave me a short lesson on the protocol of buses. The most surprising of the instructions was that he told me I need to avoid brushing my chest against fellow passengers as this can be seen as provocative. I can hold my stomach in but I have not yet managed to find a way of flattening my chest at will on a bus or any other place. I don't currently plan to get buses when travelling alone. I mostly can't even read the half-absent LED route number displayed, even if there is one.

<u>The city tour bus</u>

This can be a good option if you want comfort and the ability to hop on and off at different points, particularly if you want to see what is available in a number of different shopping centres. The city bus costs 5CUC and lasts for the day. There are two routes which both leave the Central Park, one going eastwards towards the beaches and the other heading over through Miramar as far as the Hotel Comodoro on 84th Street. It is worth noting that the two routes cross at Central Park but the tickets, at least when I last attempted to transfer, were not valid for both circuits.

<u>Private taxis</u>

These are the yellow, modern, air-conditioned cabs to be found on official taxi ranks. They have meters and are paid in CUCs.

It is also possible to pick up your own private taxi by flagging it on the street. These are usually yellow and black and very often old Ladas. I understand Cubans may pay for these in Cuban pesos but as a foreigner the drivers, like market stallholders, are likely to spot you and identify your ability to pay in CUCs. The prices for these really are best negotiated before your journey starts.

As a foreigner, expect to get the consequences of not negotiating a price before getting in. Once you have arrived at your destination, you can leave everyone with a bad taste by giving less than requested or you can avoid the situation by sorting it earlier.

In January 2015 some friends of friends, both Spanish speakers, arrived from the UK and I gave them instructions and some Cuban pesos to be able to jump into a *botero* for a trip that would take around 25 minutes. I've done it many times and pay around

50p ($20MN). With two of them it should have been a total of 40 CUP or $1.6USD. They felt rather overwhelmed by the scramble to identify the correct old car that ran that route and opted for a non-metered taxi who charged them $15. I was horrified. The most I had heard a British tourist family pay to the same location was $10, and there were five of them. If you're willing to observe and put into practice some of what you see, particularly if you have the support of a Cuban, transport is a key way of saving or overspending. But then you may want to stay in and around a walkable radius of Old Havana or Vedado (I would always recommend exploring, anyway).

Boteros

A large percentage of the old American cars are used as multi-passenger taxis. These are paid in Cuban pesos and cost 10pesos (MN) per trip. On certain routes it is now common practice for a longer journey to cost 20 pesos, particularly once through the tunnel on Línea to Miramar and the Playa district, if heading out of central Havana.

How these work is as follows: you flag down a car and state your destination. If the driver has that on his route, he'll usually just nod and you jump in, or climb, at times risking ripping your light cotton clothes on exposed springs, depending on the state of repair of the car. As you approach your destination, you tell the driver where you want him to drop you, you pay your 10 pesos and scramble out. En route other people are doing the same so there are often frequent stops. You have to know where you are going and you have to pay attention to where you are to make sure you get out at the right place.

Most tourists do not have the chance to experience this side of the American car experience, being directed to the cars that are beautifully painted and lovingly restored, and of course much more expensive as they are private contractors and paid for in tens of CUCs.

The *almendrones/ máquinas* (old American cars) are used as an alternative to buses although of course the experience differs in various senses, not least because you know that you get a seat in the "*máquina*", and there is usually the same amount of conversation. Usually none. They are driven by "*boteros*".

"Boteros" are the guys who drive this type of taxi. My use of "guys" is not sexist, nor is it used in the sense of "you guys" meaning everyone, male and female, present. I say the guys driving them because I have yet to see a woman "*boteando*". In much the same way as street taxi drivers in all the countries I know are more commonly male due to safety risks, there is the additional difficulty of the risk of breakdown and those trained in mechanics to be able to resolve engine problems, while not exclusively, again tend to be male.

Taxi rutero

This is a different experience, costing half or less of what the big old *boteros* charge, and considerably more expensive (at 5CUP) than the standard bus although they follow the bus route. You do not need to be at a bus stop to flag them down although many people are when they get bored of waiting for their bus.

This form of transport is considerably more luxurious than the bus. The routes are run by a cooperative and the 20-seater coaches are air-conditioned with signs on the outside saying that they are authorised only to carry seated passengers. Public shared transport being the most usual for most Cubans, understandably this is not always adhered to.

Whether on a bus or a *taxi rutero* it is commonplace for a younger male to give up his seat to an older woman, but while men of my own age are generally quick to offer their seat to a woman, I admit I have seen this less amongst what someone of my age might call the youth of today.

MOMENT NINETEEN

Freedom of speech

I've heard many people in Spain and the UK express an understanding they have that Cubans are at risk of committing a political crime if they express their true thoughts on the Government and the system.

From my personal experience, I can neither confirm nor rebut this notion as I have never witnessed anyone taking part in any anti-government protests. That said, I have heard many individuals express frustration with aspects of the system that they perceive do not work and they do not seem afraid to say so. I have seen many people particularly in Spain take part in mass demonstrations against Government cuts and this undoubtedly gives some semblance of popular involvement. However, I have yet to see any significant result from the people's mass protests in the UK or Spain being valuable in effecting any important result, apart from a tightening grip from the police. The same could be said in relation to the Occupy movement in the UK and the U.S., or 15-M in Spain.

The Cuban Government's updating programme, begun in 2010, has, on the other hand, made steps to respond to the needs of the people, with a series of meetings and votes at local level to determine which policies the people want and which they reject. It is a slow process but one which is progressing.

Despite what is happening at Government level, I have seen and heard many examples of artists reflecting the mood of the people and social realities through music and film.

Key examples which come to mind are Cuban rappers *Los Aldeanos*, although I admit I have never heard them on Cuban radio. I know quite a few Cubans who have heard them and I understand they have played gigs in Havana. I am not familiar with all their songs but some of the ones I have heard are very critical of the current state of the country. One of the band members is the son of a hugely popular (inside and outside Cuba) singer, Silvio Rodríguez. The word on the street is that this has provided some sort of defence from police and political silencing. Again I have no evidence.

Another singer-songwriter, Tony Ávila, many of whose lyrics make reference to the reality of life in Cuba, takes a more participatory stand. One example of this is his song *"Mi casa punto CU"* (my home.CU) in which the message is clear albeit allegorical, saying his house needs an overhaul, and he is going to get people in to do the paintwork and other jobs but without affecting the foundations. Another song of his, *El Balsero*, recognises the reality of the many Cubans who have made efforts to leave the country on makeshift rafts, facing the treacherous and shark-ridden waters of the 90 miles across the water to Florida. He does not criticise these people, acknowledging that they are doing what they think is best for themselves in their lives to move up the ladder, although his lyrics also reflect a position held by many people who want to remain in their own country.

The topic of illegal immigration has also frequently been dealt with in film. They highlight the desire to leave, sometimes bordering on desperation, combined with the negative impacts of doing so. Some focus on the dream of a new life, whether or not well-informed or realistic. Others draw out the sense of loss, particularly for the loved ones left behind and the families divided by such emigration.

MOMENT TWENTY

Sexual freedom

Cuban cinema has dealt with sensitive subjects in this regard, from *Fresa y Chocolate*'s (1994) early cinematic comments on homosexuality, through to the 2014 film "*Vestido de Novia*", highlighting some of the prejudices faced by transvestites and transgenders. Many related issues of gender and sexuality have been tackled by the film industry, including sex tourism, with leading roles played by the *jineteras,* the Cuban equivalent of prostitutes, the word having something to do with horse-riding, if you get my drift.

In my experience in Old Havana one is almost as likely to see transvestites as *jineteras*, the companions so apparently popular with tourists, although the latter are more overtly identifiable than the former given how bored they often look. *Jineterismo* is not legal although a blind eye often appears to be turned and as long as the young ladies cannot be accused of harassing tourists or obviously soliciting for business they seem to be left alone. Understandably, the old legacy of sex, drugs and gambling is one the current Administration continues to deplore and avoid.

In terms of sexual tolerance, however, Cuba has been very progressive in certain areas. In approved cases sex change processes are offered within the public health service. The country's Socialist philosophy underpinning the Revolution acknowledges equality of rights for sexual expression and CENESEX (National Centre for Sexual Education), a centre headed by Dr Mariela Castro Espín, President Raúl Castro's daughter, has as part of its remit the task of developing tolerance for the expression of sexuality. As yet, however, same-sex marriage is not currently permitted in Cuba. The issue of sexual tolerance is, in my opinion, one which draws to the forefront the dichotomy between human responses to what is seen as unnatural by many in a country which is traditionally *machista* while at the same time honouring human and social principles associated with freedom of sexual expression. From my observations there are many men who privately mock homosexuals although they do not criticise them, recognising their right to express themselves however they choose, very much in line, one might argue, with Socialist values.

Nonetheless, as is the case everywhere, one can legislate for equality and tolerance. Inherited belief systems of appropriate cultural behaviour do not necessarily adhere to legal requirements. One can only attempt to heighten awareness of the issues and encourage acceptance. One area in which this is being addressed directly is in cases of domestic violence, with Cuban institutions raising awareness of aggression in the home whether directed at women or men. I have no evidence of this being a more serious problem in Cuba than in any other country but I am aware of it being tackled in Cuba in the spirit of equality and tolerance, again in line with Socialist principles.

I know there are male nurses and female tax inspectors. I have even now seen a female taxi driver although not in charge of one of the big old American cars. There is a Federation of Cuban Women, set up by Wilma Espín, Raúl Castro's female companion during the days of the Sierra Maestra struggle in the 1950s, and mother to his children. Their daughter, Mariela Castro Espín, more recently established the Cenesex centre, focusing more specifically on raising awareness of matters around sexual orientation, expression and equality, including LBGT and related gender issues, rather than solely women's rights.

MOMENT TWENTY-ONE

Holidays

Many tourists have visited Cuba and enjoyed its climate, its music, its beaches, its museums, and, although it might not be politically correct to mention it, its decay, its slowness, its paralysis. Any holiday for someone from the so-called developed world is a break from the rushed life, the tedium, the pressures. One could call it an escape. And this section is not about holidays for foreigners in Cuba. It is about the holidays Cubans take.

The first thing to note is that they have a right to a month's holiday per year.

Second, is that they often use this time to just stay at home and be with family. Many of them do not leave home to take a holiday. There are various reasons for this. One is that it is not part of their usual practice. Another is cost although some from Havana will rent a place by the beach for a week in the summer. They are the privileged ones.

In line with socialist principles, some organisations offer subsidised holidays to workers as an acknowledgement of their contribution. These may include days out with co-workers or a week at the beach in the summer. Always, of course, in Cuba.

Some visit family members in other parts of the country. However, to go in a comfortable air-conditioned bus from Havana to Trinidad for example costs $25CUCs each way and this is more than a month's wages for many State workers. Some self-employed people may have access to that but they are less likely to want to take time away from work. What becomes a holiday for many is a visit from a family member who is living abroad and returns with the children for example to see the grandparents and the cousins. They of course bring hard currency which affords some luxuries.

Some Cubans with family members or close friends overseas have been able to visit for extended stays. It almost goes without saying that this is as long as the inviting sponsor covers all costs. A State worker's monthly salary will very often not even cover the cost of a taxi to the airport. Even when invited by a sponsor, travel may be blocked on imagined grounds that the Cuban will almost certainly be at risk of overstaying their visa, irrespective of statements made. This lack of trust appears to be institutional.

MOMENT TWENTY-TWO

Travel opportunities for Cubans

There is a widely-held misconception that the Cuban government does not allow United States citizens to visit the island, nor does it allow Cuban nationals to travel abroad, perhaps without renouncing their Cuban citizenship.

Neither of these contentions is correct, although the latter belief has its roots in past, now superseded legislation. Well, not totally. In the UK, we have ten-year passports. In Cuba, passports, which are paid for in CUCs, are for a maximum of six years. There is a further limitation. They have to be updated every two years, by paying a supplement. Fortunately it does not have to be the exact date, which would seriously limit flexibility of travel plans, but it does ensure that Cubans who maintain property in Cuba while living abroad fulfil the requirement to return at least once in two years. As a deterrent to the pre-revolutionary practice of speculative property purchase, with landlords living abroad and potentially pushing up rents for local people on the island, Cuba does not allow ownership of more than one property and requires regular return to the island.

This was previously a bit more restrictive as Cubans living abroad were required to have an overseas residence permit. This required annual return to their homes to retain property rights. That has changed as part of Raúl's updating programme.

For a UK tourist to travel to Cuba they have to obtain a tourist visa. If the tourist is planning on staying with family members they are required to alter their status via the local immigration office once in Cuba (a current cost of $40) so as to ensure income from home stays is declared and corresponding taxes paid.

A U.S. citizen is required by her own Government to obtain a licence to travel to Cuba. Famously Beyoncé did this in 2013 and drew criticism from various quarters, in part due to U.S. legislation under which Cuba was classified as a State Sponsor of Terrorism. The Patriot Act states that any U.S. citizens paying anything direct to Cubans in Cuba, whether a tip in a bar or a taxi ride, is legally defined as trading with the enemy. President Obama's declarations at the end of 2014 and early 2015 have expanded the categories under which North American citizens can apply for a licence and lifted some restrictions on travel to Cuba for U.S. citizens, as well as opening the door for the U.S. to reconsider its designation of Cuba as a State sponsoring terrorism.

In fact President Obama finally proposed to Congress that the designation be lifted and on 29 May 2015, the following was posted on the Whitehouse blog[4]:

Rescission of Cuba as a State Sponsor of Terrorism

Posted by Bernadette Meehan on May 29, 2015 at 12:33 PM EDT

In December 2014, when the President announced our historic shift in Cuba policy, he opened a new era in our relationship with the Cuban people, and the entire hemisphere. The President's new approach to Cuba moves beyond decades of unsuccessful efforts to isolate Cuba, and is the continuation of a process designed to empower the Cuban people. This dramatically improves our capacity to promote the interests and democratic values that the United States stands for across the Americas and around the globe.

As part of our new way forward with Cuba, the President in December instructed the Secretary of State to immediately launch a review of Cuba's designation as a State Sponsor of Terrorism, and conclude that review within six months. In April, the Secretary of State completed that review and recommended to the President that Cuba should no longer be designated as a State Sponsors of Terrorism. The President then submitted to Congress the statutorily required report indicating the Administration's intent to rescind Cuba's State Sponsor of Terrorism designation, including the certification that Cuba has not provided any support for international terrorism during the previous six-months; and that Cuba has provided assurances that it will not support acts of international terrorism in the future.

The 45-day Congressional pre-notification period is now complete and we are pleased to note that today the Secretary of State has rescinded Cuba's designation as a State Sponsor of Terrorism.

The rescission of Cuba's designation as a State Sponsor of Terrorism reflects our assessment that Cuba meets the statutory criteria for rescission. While the United States has significant concerns and disagreements with a wide range of Cuba's policies and actions, these fall outside the criteria relevant to the rescission of a state sponsor of terrorism designation.

So that is presumably good news if you are going to work in Cuba.

The Cuban authorities have required you to have a different type of visa according to whether or not you are being contracted by a locally registered company. This latter type of visa, in my experience, can take a long time to process and be issued. It is also my understanding that it is very difficult, drawn out and costly to attempt to change a tourist visa to a work visa once in the country.

The other side of the coin is travel opportunities for Cubans. What has often been in the way of them travelling abroad is the entry restrictions imposed by host countries. As far as I can tell, mostly visas are refused on the grounds that the visa issue officer is not satisfied that the applicant will return to Cuba. That is maybe a reasonable concern given the low economic levels in the country. However, I have witnessed one visa being refused on the grounds that the applicant only earns the equivalent of £5.67 per month and it is deemed cannot sustain himself in the UK, despite his girlfriend having submitted documentary evidence of employment and home ownership, plus testimony to the fact she was willing to cover all travel and subsistence costs incurred during his visit. If visas were only given to people who could support themselves in the U.K., we would have to assume that an extraordinarily small number of Cubans would ever be given an entry visa for any country unless they were engaging in a government-sponsored activity, and maybe not even then.

In recent years when Cuba lifted its requirement for Cubans to apply for a permit to travel outside Cuba, a number of other countries reportedly tightened their visa restrictions. Notable was Ecuador, which had previously not required Cubans to have a visa. An unexpected move from Evo Morales who has been such a supporter of Cuba in international fora.

As regards Cubans being able to travel, Cuba's government institutionalised some restrictions on Cubans leaving the homeland in order to respond to active recruitment policies from their North American neighbours which put Cuba at risk of losing many of its professionals who had received free education in Cuba only to be seduced overseas to work, particularly in the highly-paid health sector, a strategy which was a way of undermining the Cuban political system and society, thereby collapsing the regime, or so it was apparently intended.

MOMENT TWENTY-THREE

Cuban-Cuban relations

Being with a Cuban in Cuba, and possibly more so with a black Cuban, has given me an insight into some responses of Cubans that I would prefer not to have had, and maybe they are all understandable within a country where the people are so used to the "us and them" syndrome, so perhaps a Cuban with a white foreigner draws attention and a different relationship amongst one's own countrymen.

My white western appearance has not once triggered a challenge from any hotel security staff when I have entered alone. Yet with my husband we have been asked on a number of occasions if we are residents in a hotel that we might be visiting to have a drink, use the internet, or enter one of their shops. Being a hotel resident is not a requirement for any of those activities or justifications for being on hotel premises.

It's true that until maybe ten years ago or less Cubans were not permitted to enter tourist hotels. I remember a friend of mine years ago telling me he had come to Cuba to scuba-dive and that there was a wire fence at the entry to Varadero, only allowing Cubans who were working in the local hospitality industry to enter. That was one of the aspects that put me off going sooner as I thought I would be restricted to that area and not be allowed to experience what some might call "the real Cuba". If there was ever that restriction for foreigners, it no longer exists. I have been able to wander wherever I have chosen, even if sometimes we are asked questions.

So now Cubans can enter freely and do what other hotel guests do, consume. The only restriction as ever is of course their ability to pay in CUCs. In one hotel we went to the roof terrace and a doorman who took his job overly seriously (what I call a "jobsworth") accused my then fiancé of going to the rooms, a challenge to which he simply responded by asking the guy if he was sure that what he was saying was true. With no aggression, voice-raising or further intervention, the doorman ended up apologising for his mistake (which he realised he'd made) and the pair of them shaking hands.

My husband had never previously associated with non-Cubans for no reason except that the opportunity had never presented itself and he was employed in a field that did not bring him into contact with them, so occasionally he himself has been irritated by the attitude of some of his countrymen towards him when he is with me. He almost always does the shopping at the market so the vendors don't see a foreigner and underweigh or overprice. With what appears to be a growing number of foreigners taking up residence in Cuba, often engaging in the hospitality business with their Cuban partners or associates, a few extra pesos can be made from those like me who are not going to get into an argument about how many lemons one can expect in a pound.

Certain places, such as the Marina Hemingway leisure complex, where we spent our honeymoon, is patrolled by officious security guards who, as far as I can tell, almost always start to speak with a tone of accusation because they seem to assume that they are dealing with a Cuban who is making money from hanging out with a female tourist, and they almost always assume the right to tell us we have no right to be walking by the quayside. I enjoy seeing them recoil when I intervene in Spanish or my husband affords the minimum amount of information but makes it clear he has as much right as me or any other visitor to stroll where he fancies. At least the owners of sizeable yachts can be confident that they will not receive interference from any grubby locals during their stopover.

Similarly, during our last visit, we phoned to check the details of an activity at a club we belong to that caters primarily for foreigners. The telephonist wasted a considerable amount of my husband's phone credit by asking where he was from and mistakenly stating they didn't have any Cuban members. She could have just answered the question as asked. She scurried off to confirm our membership with a colleague before answering the question. She did not offer an apology for questioning my husband's word.

There is a frequently commented attitude that is expressed in some songs I have heard[5] which reflects a view that if someone chooses to travel in any way apart from on a humanitarian mission or for lectures overseas for example, that s/he is in some way betraying

---

[5] Los Aldeanos: Hotel Nacional; Tony Ávila: Balsero

the Revolution. This seems to be a justification for some Cubans to treat other Cubans with less respect. Or it could just be envy as their opportunities have been expanded. Or maybe fear as they think someone who has travelled or married a foreigner is anti-Revolutionary and therefore a threat, or at least a potential threat. I cannot comment further on that as I doubt anyone would admit it. And in any case, it is distant from the truth. Maybe it's not even deliberate. It's just something that can be observed and experienced. And both I and my husband have observed and experienced it. These attitudes, whatever it is they are based on, will undoubtedly take time to enter the consciousness of the whole of Cuban society and adapt.

MOMENT TWENTY-FOUR

Drinking water

I have not yet met anyone from Havana who claims that it is safe to drink tap water in the city. I cannot confirm this is the case in other parts of the country. However, since the problem exists primarily because of the water storage systems in buildings, common throughout Cuba, I would expect the same condition to pertain.

Just about every rooftop you see in the city has water tanks, different sizes, different colours, and apparently in different weathered states. The water comes in from the main pipes and it is stored for one very good reason. Water in some parts of the city is turned off at certain times of the day so you need a storage system so you access whenever you want. Of course, the roof tank system makes it far less appealing for drinking.

For tourists, buying bottled water is a common solution when travelling abroad and not considered to be a huge expense, or at least not an extravagance. When living in Cuba on something similar to a Cuban salary, the expense of buying mineral water is considerable and beyond the budget. So tap water is boiled and decanted into plastic bottles. You can imagine our place in Cuba has an ever-increasing store of used soda and cola bottles.

A phenomenon which would not affect individual residences, but which can cause difficulties in multi-residence apartments blocks is that the water pumps drawing down from the rooftop tanks are sometimes turned off at night. My experience in one such building was that this process was not regulated by a timer but by a person, meaning that the whole of the block had to adapt to his/her schedule, i.e. the water went off around midnight and came back on around 6a.m., or 8a.m. at weekends, a real inconvenience when I wanted to get up and out and be fresh after a night of humidity-accompanied restlessness replacing sleep. Most foreigners travelling or working in Cuba will probably not have to deal with such inconveniences but if you are dealing with Cubans it is as well to be aware of *their* circumstances in order to reach a better understanding of their lives and needs.

My previous experience in relation to domestic water was undoubtedly similar to that of most of the other residents in our block. We shared the inconvenience. The water pumps were not regulated by each apartment. And many, or maybe most, of the apartments did not have independent water heaters, meaning that while the kitchen sink, the bathroom hand basin, and the shower all had mixer taps, the only thing to come out of any of them was cold water, heated by the sun on the pipework on the many days that happened, and in the winter coming out at the temperature you would expect cold water to come out of a cold tap. Cold. Not the sort of freezing cold spewed from the cold tap in England, but not warm enough to shower under on a cold day in Cuba.

So the Cuban solution, maybe familiar in other countries with similar circumstances: you boil the water. Logical. You then carry the bucket of water through to the shower, add some cold, use whatever receptacle you have to spill the water over your head and body, and then just refresh the skin with a cold water rinse. Just as well that cold in Cuba isn't freezing.

I don't know about everybody's house but, given the cost of everything in Cuba, and the fact that there is a general assumption that everything has more than one function, what we used for the shower was a plastic one-litre ice-cream tub. We ate the ice-cream first. Nestlé always accompanied us to the bathroom. We always half-filled one of their tubs for brushing teeth. My favourite was the fudge flavour. A practical solution. We took no risks with bugs in the water. Even in the water we were going to be spitting out. I would take a guess that high-class hotels have an adequate filtration system but there was no guarantee of that in our building, so I even took to pre-boiling the water I used in my coffee pot even though it was going to boil again as it percolated. That was a way of limiting my stomach's reaction to everything new.

MOMENT TWENTY-FIVE

Everything has its use

Not related to the water situation, but definitely related to the multiple uses of almost everything in Cuba, I recall on my first visit when I was completely unaware of many aspects of life there. (Yes, I know I say that as if it's no longer true). I was invited to my friend's brother's birthday party and they had prepared a large pot of a stew-like soup to share (*caldosa*). I admit to having been somewhat shocked by the fact that it was served in ice-cream pots. I thought they must be very poor to not be able to buy plates. This was of course grounded in my ignorance of the cost of a plate or a dish as a percentage of a standard monthly income. But it still felt strange to me supping soup from an ice-cream pot.

Progress happens somehow and in my own house, we now have four dinner plates. When we have had the family round for a meal, we have borrowed plates from the neighbour. It's not too much of a problem as she is related to my in-laws so has been one of the guests anyway. When this hasn't been the case, we have simply eaten in shifts. At my brother-in-law's house, shifts are the order of the day as he tends to invite quite a few people and the table can only really seat four at a time, so, like most things in Cuba, solutions are found.

There's a saying in Cuba that "he who hangs on to things, always has what he needs". Given how frequently one looks in the shops for things that we find are temporarily unavailable, one has to sympathise with this attitude. The downside, or one of them, is that in our house we have a room full of stuff that doesn't work. Maybe one day one part of an old piece of tat will be used in something else. Meanwhile, there it is filling up the space. We're just lucky to have more space than some people.

MOMENT TWENTY-SIX

Eating out in Cuba

This is one of my favourite activities although it is one which is not frequently affordable to the majority of Cubans.

There is plenty of choice. I have been told by other foreigners who came to Cuba ten years ago that the food was not up to much. But, as with many things in Cuba, this has changed.

If you are in an all-inclusive hotel you will most likely find an abundance of the standard international cuisine presented in an eat-as-much-as-you-want buffet format. The rules of this will most likely depend on whether there are a lot of Cubans resident in the hotel. If so, (and I want Cubans to forgive me for saying this, it is what I observe not what I judge, and I understand the background scarcity conversation) you will probably find that they will collect their starter, main course and dessert all in the initial visit to the counter. It surprised me at first. And I judged it as greedy and inappropriate. And as I have understood more, I have come to consider it as a normal response in a country where you can select as much as you want from a huge spread of food is so uncommon. It seems as Cuba is a country where if you don't take what you are offered when you are offered it, you may well lose the chance. I have seen this on many an occasion. Cubans know it. Cuban comedians have mentioned it.

I have also seen a skit on how a Cuban will guard their shopping trolley even before they have paid for their items. My husband has done this in the UK. The action is clearly related to the fear that someone will want what you have in your basket and in the time it has taken you to get to the check-out, whatever it was has you took from the shelf may have by now sold out.

On the subject of selling out, it is not unusual to turn up at a restaurant and be told that something or other, despite being on the menu, is not available. This was the case with chips and potatoes for 2 months at the beginning of 2015. Happily, they re-appeared in the markets before February was out.

Privately owned restaurants have become a very popular sector of activity amongst Cubans who have decided to take advantage of the 2010 stimulus for self-employed status. The best of these will tell you if anything is not available at the moment they hand you the menu. This of course is best for someone like me to avoid unnecessary salivation at the thought of such culinary delights as lobster, king prawns and lamb steaks. "Havana's Good Food Guide" may not yet have been written but there is an ever-increasing availability of excellent venues and dishes. The "What's on in Havana" online monthly internet brochure does, however, include some brief comments on popular and recommended places to eat in different districts of the city.

Personally I would generally avoid them though as they are where most foreigners are likely to conglomerate, but they may be of interest to some.

What you will find is that you will most probably be eating in restaurants where prices are in CUCs. That said, in January 2015 I went with my husband to a pizza restaurant on Calle 23 in Vedado and was surprised and delighted to enjoy 2 tasty pizzas and 2 fresh fruit salads and a creamy soup all for 43CUP (less than £1.20) for the two of us. At those prices and with that quality, it's no surprise that we were queuing outside for the best part of an hour, although many other days I have passed I have not seen that level of popularity. Unsurprisingly it is patronised almost exclusively by Cubans, who are, of course, very used to queueing, as we will see.

MOMENT TWENTY-SEVEN

Queues: how to manage and avoid them

I can't remember if I read it or was told but I know that at some stage (very early on) I learned that if there is a queue, the best thing to do in Cuba is join it first then find out later what is on offer. Sometimes queues even start forming before anything is available and when you ask "What's the queue for?" they may well say "Whatever there is".

I found this practice useful when I was first working there and didn't want people to be able to spot straight away from my accent that I was foreign. So I didn't ask. I kept my mouth shut in the hope I could blend with the queue and I just did what the Cubans do.

For that reason, on my way home from work one day, I spotted a queue and joined it. I then watched what people who had reached the front were carrying away. As it turned out on that occasion, it was for bread. No problem. We can always freeze it if my husband has bought some too. So I stayed in line for another 15 minutes or so until I reached the counter. I asked for my two loaves and was told that what was available was not for general sale. It was the "*libreta*" quota. I was not able to buy it unless I had my basic foods book (the *libreta*) with me. My employer had still not, after two months, sorted out my paperwork so I walked away from the counter with no food except for thought. I guessed for some that the lengthy bread queue was a daily occurrence until I discovered that the oven had been broken for a few days so there had been a backlog on that particular occasion.

Other queues I have had the pleasure of joining have included when I wanted to buy the washing machine. It turned out that the place where we were going to buy it had had a delivery of the TV digi-box. There are still plenty of people who do not have that pearl of equipment, so when they appear in the stores there is a dash for them and to the latest queue. No such luxury in the store as one person dealing with that and others dealing with other purchases. Nooo. Just wait in line until each person has their own individual introduction to how the digi-box works, checks that there are no pieces missing, counts out the cash and has a social interaction with half a dozen people standing by.

Once that process is complete, you get to the front of the queue to have your own interaction about the washing machine you want to buy, all the time hoping that it won't get so late that you'll get caught up in the increasing traffic and will manage to find a taxi to be able to get this heavy piece of domestic kit home. The taxi of course has to be driven by someone young and fit enough to be able to help my husband lift it in and then get it up the stairs to our flat. It also has to be sufficiently big and sturdy to not be overladen by the weight. The joyful anticipation of our own washing machine being installed in our flat kept me smiling during the whole apparently interminable wait on the wall outside the shop, guarding the new purchase, while my husband went off in search of the appropriate transport at the appropriate negotiated price.

A Cuban in Cuba said to me a couple of years ago that Cubans have very little of pretty much everything. Except time. If you plan to achieve very little in a day, then you will not be subject to the kind of frustration that I have at times indulged. Back in the UK I can count on distances taking a certain amount of time in my car and can plan to see more than one friend in an afternoon. It doesn't tend to work that way in Havana.

The day we bought the washing machine was just like many others in the capital. So let's take a look at the detail.

My husband arranged to take his mother to the neurological specialist in the morning. This arrangement had involved him going the previous week and securing an appointment, scheduled for 7.30am. He made plans. His brother came to collect him (in his works van) after collecting his 88-year old mother, at 7am. I received a text message from my husband at 12.42 saying that they had still not seen the doctor, and there were people ahead of them in the queue. They finally saw the specialist at 4.15pm.

I have not learned yet to overcome my bewilderment at the level of skill and patience that has to be exercised to operate anything, not least public health services, with such a level of systematic unworkability. Or maybe the unworkability is systemic. I don't want to tempt fate by saying I need additional examples to confirm this.

Anyway, while my husband headed to the hospital, my plan involved heading to the immigration office to extend my visa, valid for a month but which can be renewed up to six months as a family member, by paying $25 and attending the office every 30 days. I had extended once already and had not remembered until that morning that the $25 has to be paid in official stamps that can be bought exclusively from banks. Kicking myself for not racing to the bank earlier, I headed off, remembering that our nearest (5 blocks away) is currently closed for refurbishment. The next nearest is 20 blocks away and of course was temporarily serving a wider area. I had promised myself I would get to the immigration office before 8.30 so I would not be faced with the inevitable ever-increasing queue. But having remembered the need for the stamps, it was 9.10 when I arrived at the bank. By then I faced a sea of bodies jumbled outside in the Cuban version of a queue.

Of course one has to know how to queue in Cu-queue-ba. It might look like a muddle but everyone who turns up to join any queue asks "¿El último?" (the last one) so they know who they are behind and who is in front of that person. Pretty much everyone knows who is in front and who is behind them, and one more in either direction, and if they get impatient or run out of time, they just tell the person behind that they can take their place. Or the practice is used to reserve your place if you need to go off to work for an hour and come back and rejoin the queue. Bizarre practices. But they work.

In fact, one guy must have seen the slowness of the queue that morning and did exactly that. I asked "el último?", a question received with a laugh from a guy who thought he was the one who arrived just before me. His chuckle was one of recognition - it didn't much matter who was the last as we were all going to be stood outside for at least a couple of hours of enforced sunbathing.

I didn't wait as I was not up for a dose of vitamin D, and I knew that if I went to immigration straight afterwards I would end up facing longer queues there. On top of that I was meeting a friend at 11am, in the sort of daft non-Cuban style of actually planning to do something else with my day in addition to what I considered to be a simple administrative process. Another note to self: next time I'll get up early and start the queue earlier.

Of course, I had to take a decision: stay in the queue in order to join another one at immigration and not see my friend, or see my friend and abandon the admin processes until the next day. I chose the latter.

When I was telling my friend, who happens to be Spanish and married to a Cuban, about my delightful queuing morning, her response was the same as that of many foreigners and Cubans alike. She flashed me a look of incomprehension at my refusal to play the trump card I always hold in this country. The metal or paper ace, which pretty much always allows you to avoid lengthy queues. Spanish not being my first language I have not yet, however, learned the look, the unspoken gesture, or the words to express "I need to get out of this sun, do my business, and get on with my life, and if you facilitate that there will be something in it for you." Of course the little tip ("*la propinita*") or little gift ("*el regalito*") is regular in Cuba. It has to be. Some people are in fact busy. Far from all Cubans can afford the time required to undertake one activity per day. Of course many others do not have the metal or paper wherewithal to be able to jump to the front.

Tipping is commonplace but a Cuban administrator once suggested to my husband that he should take a little gift to whoever he dealt with at the office where he needed to go to get another copy of an official document. He had to be careful so as not to be seen to be bribing someone. So I think he took a little carton of drink as a gift on occasions. That way you can be more subtle by pressing a dollar note or coin against the carton if you choose. And a nice chilled juice is always welcomed. It's kind of sweet but my husband is an innocent who would previously have been amongst the mass of those who have more time than disposable money so queueing was the only option. The tip however tends to help encourage the person to delay their lunch break or give you a more personalised attention by not putting your request on the same pending and inactive pile as all the others. It undoubtedly causes upset among the people who can see what it is going on but cannot play the same game. And the ones most likely to be able to play the tipping game are the foreigners. Personally, I don't want to engage in this sort of friction-building divisive practice, playing the "I can solve anything with my little bit of money because you lot are poorer than me" ploy. Sometimes I can see, though, it seems by far the easiest option.

I actually don't like admitting all of this as I fear any undiscerning readers out there might choose to criticise a system which has allowed this to happen. From my own background, I know the value of a bit of monetary encouragement. Maybe I need to check the splinter in my own eye, the one that requires me to pay for everything in my own country, to find the solutions on-line or with often unanswered, highly expensive telephone enquiry lines, usually manned by people with a script and accents I don't comprehend, or the depersonalised service that is administered by post and which can only be accelerated by paying more. People who got tangled up in the newly contracted Teleperformance-operated UK Passport Office fiasco in 2014 will know what I am talking about. I would guess that there are many who would have offered a little tip to someone to find out where their damned papers were and not have to cancel travel plans.

Queues for the bus also operate the "who am I behind?" system. Unsurprisingly my husband's patience in waiting for buses extends far beyond my own. I decided to wait for a *taxi rutero* one day and got bored after an hour. Maybe I was waiting in the wrong place but I have decided that an hour of my life is worth more than the 40p I was going to save. It was an interesting experiment and I enjoyed watching people busying themselves with central Havana life so I don't consider I wasted my time completely, which is generally how I view hanging around waiting for something, whether or not in queues.

I have just noticed what a huge number of lines I have dedicated to queuing. Maybe it is appropriate given its importance in a country where so little information is digitalised and personal attendance is the norm. Either I will get used to it or it will change. Maybe it's just a case of which happens first.

MOMENT TWENTY-EIGHT

Banks and administration

As far as I can see, the banks are amongst the best places to practise queues. If someone needs the bank, they need the bank. Some things just cannot be done elsewhere. So you can expect a queue.

The day after I had abandoned my stamp-buying in the bank, I decided to try a different branch. I figured there would be fewer people as it was not serving the people from my most local branch which was temporarily closed. It was not the best decision I have ever made.

I queued for four hours in the end.

We were told that the computer system was down. Of course, you get chatting to other more or less frustrated queuers, one of whom noticed I was English. I tend to be taken for Spanish, never

Cuban, and never before English. Anyway, one of the comments, somewhat tongue in cheek, was that the problem was caused by the friends in the north. While the guy was clearly being satirical, my mind meandered to replace the boredom of the queue. It occurred to me that if you have the technological power and expertise to regulate internet access and you have a potential interest in having it not work, then what better way to get people on your side by tinkering with their system, having it not work, and then coming in as the saviours with your promise of wider access to hi-tech global communications networks? But that is an aside. Meandering mind.

Once you get inside the bank and out of the sun, you are almost sure to be in another queue inside. In contrast, the Cadeca exchange bureaux are usually only willing to let you in once you can go straight to a counter, and in places where the most officious workers are in attendance they refuse to let anyone else in with you. My husband and I have got round this one by splitting the money we want to exchange so that both of us get to go in. When I exchange money it tends to be in amounts that I prefer to distribute between the two of us and in various pockets, and I am not going to let some power-grabber interfere with how I want to organise myself and my life. The pettiness can be a little irritating but I have gradually evolved my ability to be entertained by it and find my own responses. I do this in the UK too as a way of overcoming my irritation at petty rules and petty people who want to enforce them.

I should mention that one of the things I love about changing money in Cuba is the receipt which gives a straightforward "this for that" number and has no hidden bank theft mechanisms such as commission or differentiated rates according to where you undertake the transaction.

MOMENT TWENTY-NINE

The feria – fresh food market

The fresh food market is an experience. It only happens once every month or so, and I have not yet found out how people hear about it apart from "Radio Bemba", the local name for "word of mouth", literally "Radio Big Lips".

The lorries come in from the countryside with all their fresh produce. It's pretty specialised in that each lorry tends to have no more than 3 products for sale and many have just one, particularly the case with the bananas. The onion lorry diversifies by having red onions and white onions. Lettuces are sold from another truck.

The police are always in attendance, although mainly to redirect traffic as the whole street is dedicated to the market. That said, the New Year's Eve market was particularly frantic. A lot of products were not available and the vendors with the best looking goods got a lot of attention, with the resulting fracas and undisciplined queues. On one lorry I did see a policeman who had climbed aboard to direct the sale of the produce, although I cannot remember what. It was probably something most people wanted for their New Year's dinner and was in short supply, at least of good quality.

Of course if you go to the market you need bags to carry everything home. The lucky people who have had extra funds from whatever source have shopping trolleys with wheels. In fact, we were able to borrow one of those from our neighbour on one occasion. We were also able to borrow our nephew to assist! Happily, nothing is bought in small pre-packaged amounts. Bulk-buying is the norm as you have no idea when it's coming in again.

Other shoppers come with huge bags over their shoulders and yet more turn up with a range of contraptions with wheels able to carry various sacks but also adaptable for other purposes, the same idea as soup from ice-cream pots.

MOMENT THIRTY

Religion in Cuba

I can only comment here on certain elements that have come into my awareness through observation and asking a few questions. There are many sources which examine religious tolerance and practice in detail. I have not read most of them.

The official line is that religious practice is a constitutional right like many others.

Having inherited Catholicism as my designated religion, on account of that being the religion my parents inherited, I have no more than an academic understanding of any other religion. In fact, you could probably say that I have no more than an academic understanding of Catholicism, given that my personal view is that religion is primarily a way of encouraging its followers to think and behave in a particular manner. It can provide a certain level of social order. But that is no more or less than my personal view.

I mention it because I can only identify what I have observed and learned about religious practice, although I find the whole area totally bewildering, and intrinsically personal.

So, while I acknowledge the right to religious belief and practice, I do not pretend to understand it anywhere on the planet. In Cuba, much falls outside my own evaluative framework given that the majority religion is "Santería", a "syncretised" religion, drawing on, and interweaving elements from, the range of cultural players including the Aboriginals of the island, their Spanish colonisers, Jewish and Chinese immigrants, and the slaves imported from many different geographical locations and regional cultures who, while sharing the same skin pigmentation, did not all share the same language, cultural heritage, or religious practices.

I believe this sincretised religion, "Santería", is exclusive to Cuba. I am not aware of it being practised anywhere else.

You will see churches. There are many in Cuba. I haven't spotted any that have been turned into cafés or climbing-wall centres, as you get in the UK, though. I have seen Catholic churches, Baptist, Methodist and Seventh-day Adventist places of worship. There are Jehovah's Witnesses in Cuba, Muslims and Jews. Nobody has ever tried to persuade me of the benefit of their own religious beliefs. I have a choice.

If I want religious icons, there is no shortage of places to buy them. Many of the souvenir shops sell brightly coloured religious images and plaques depicting the most prominent Santería gods: Eleggua (black and red, depicted as a child, god of the paths); Yemayá (white and blue, woman, goddess of the sea); Changó (red and white, man, god of fire); Ochún (yellow and white, woman, goddess of the rivers); and Obbatalá (white, man, god of universal wisdom).

There is a part of the Malecón near the mouth of the Almendares river where I have often seen people invoking the power of Yemayá and making offerings. I have spotted bunches of flowers, shoes and dead birds tucked into the roots or crevices of trees on random streets, and I have been told not to look too closely, apparently so as not to invoke the "evil eye", potentially interfering with a deeply spiritual experience of another. My own inherited Irish culture taught me a different version of all these practices, often akin to superstitions, so I can observe them from a distance and respect them while not being emotionally involved with them.

One of the most striking features of religious practice for me is the people dressed entirely in white, male and female, some young, although of many different ages. This includes white umbrellas and parasols, white shoes and white hats. My understanding is that these people are in a year-long preparation to celebrate becoming an officially recognised disciple of a particular "saint", a significant rite of passage in Santería. Maybe they become saints in the process. I don't yet have a grasp on that one.

It occurred to me that in a country where people wait so long for buses so as not to pay the comparatively high prices for taxi services, the visits of our flower lady might seem a little excessive. She cycles by every day so maybe she always has customers. I have wondered how people have money for flowers so regularly. The mind meanders again and I wonder if it could be a result of people wanting to make an offering to one or other of the gods to help them deal with an illness or an adversity they or a loved one is facing. I cannot confirm this, but I do know that offerings are often made even by some who do not adhere regularly to religious practice but may be challenged by a particular circumstance at a given time and feel the need for any type of support, real or imagined.

I have also met some who have advised me not to believe any of this, what they have called, hocus-pocus. There have undoubtedly been cases where the spiritual guides *(babalaos)*, who may have suggested a particular offering, have sometimes included a requirement to make an offering of a chicken, or other food, to be delivered to the spiritual guide himself. It's like saying, offer it up to the gods, but since they can't eat it, offer some of it to me and I'll ensure the gratitude is transmitted. And yes, the "Babalao" is always male, not accepting, in the same way as Catholics, women into this rank of seniority.

One observation I have with regard to religion is that there does not appear to be any religious practice or belief which is <u>expected</u> from other family members. In the same family, there could be a parent who declares him/herself as Catholic, another parent without any expressed religious belief, a son who believes all religious practice is nonsense, another who is doing what needs to be done to become a *babalao*, and another who is willing to make offerings without engaging in the other aspects of religious practice. This is very different from my own background where families tend to pass on their religious beliefs in much the same way as a surname is adopted.

MOMENT THIRTY-ONE

Theatre, cinema and culture

I love going to the cinema in Cuba. You can take your popcorn if you want and there are regular screenings in many local cinemas, often with two showings per day. One of the things I like best is that it is so cheap. If I go to the cinema in the UK, it will probably cost me around £8 per ticket, I may have to pay for parking, and any refreshments I buy will be sugar-fuelled and expensive.

In Cuba, many of the films are shown in the original version with Cubans having to read sub-titles in Spanish. Nevertheless, everyone has enough money to go to the cinema. There are many theatres too and attendance is supported by the prices. The cinema costs from one to five pesos (MN), so around 10p, and the theatre costs 10 pesos (MN) for Cubans and Cuban residents. Some theatres do have differentiated prices for foreigners. A recent case was 10 pesos (MN) for Cubans and 10CUC for foreigners, so a massive difference but it does mean that even foreigners can attend a top ballet performance for around £6.50, a fraction of London prices where theatre-going is a pleasure to be enjoyed by those with enough money to be classed as elite.

Many of the excellent music concerts I have attended in Havana have been in the open-air and with absolutely no entrance fee. Music, art and cultural expression are viewed in Cuba as integral to a cultured society.

MOMENT THIRTY-TWO

Heroes in Cuba

Reference is often made in Cuba to national heroes. You will see busts of the philosophical inspiration for the Revolution, José Martí Pérez, in every school and on many streets. You will notice enormous images of revolutionaries Ernesto "Che" Guevara and Camilo Cienfuegos on the walls of ministry buildings in Revolution Square, as well as paintings of them on walls round Havana's city centre. Korda's photo of "Che" has been reproduced on clothes, books and many souvenirs. If you recognise Julio Antonio Mella, the leader of the revolutionary student movement executed at 27 years of age, you will spot him around too.

I truly believe that it is impossible to comprehend Cuba's Revolution and the people's willingness to cope with the difficulties of life unless you are familiar with the country's struggle for independence, first from the colonial power of Spain and then from the imperial domination intended by the U.S.

There are key figures who have played significant roles in this struggle, amongst whom José Martí is probably the most widely acknowledged due to his writings. His complete works are compiled in 27 volumes. On account of him being hailed as the philosophical leader of the Revolution, he holds a hero status after being killed in combat in 1895, at the relatively young age of 42.

More recent heroes of Cuba are "The Cuban Five" or "*Los Cinco*": Gerardo Hernández Nordelo, Ramón Labañino Salazar, René González Sehwerert, Antonio Guerrero Rodríguez and Fernando González Llort. They were detained in the U.S. back in 1998. Many people were concerned about the absence of a fair trial, allegations of bribes and threats to witnesses, and a lack of evidence on which their severe sentences were based.

There was an international movement demanding their freedom. Key websites devoted to their cause included www.freethefive.org and http://www.thecuban5.org website. Back in December 2001, Fidel Castro conferred the title of "Hero of the Republic of Cuba" on each of the five anti-terrorists and insistently declared "They will return".

For years, the newspaper *Granma* carried adverts with details on how to contact "The Five" to write with messages of solidarity and encouragement. René González was the first to be released in October 2011, although he was placed on probation in the U.S. for a further three years and unable to return to Cuba. He was allowed to return to Cuba for his father's funeral in April 2013, and a federal judge allowed him to stay there provided that he renounce his United States citizenship.

Next was Fernando González Llort, who completed his prison sentence in February 2014 and was returned to Cuba the next day. In March 2014 *Preliminary conclusions of the Commission of Inquiry* were presented after a meeting held in London, which René González was unable to attend on account of his visa application being turned down by the British authorities. He participated via Skype from Cuba. An extract from the Preliminary Conclusions can be found printed at the end of this book.

After spending years in prison in the U.S., the release of the last three being announced by the U.S. in December 2014 was a celebrated fulfilment of Fidel Castro's 2001 prophecy. Replacing the posters encouraging Cubans to remember their compatriots, found in places like the bus station, you will now see posters celebrating their return to the homeland.

You will not see any statues of Fidel Castro as the leader of the Revolution. Apparently, it is not deemed as appropriate as it would constitute a form of homage to a person who is still alive, and such hero worship of the living does not fit with their Socialist principles.

The dead are a different matter. Particularly if they died in battle. Names like Antonio Maceo and Carlos Manuel de Céspedes, key players in the fight for independence from Spain in the 19th century, are familiar to all Cubans and their hero status has even been embodied in language with phrases acknowledging their courage and their part in the struggle for sovereignty.

Commemorating the living and the dead, on 24th February 2015, coinciding with the 120th anniversary of the *Grito de Baire*, one of the early demonstrations of the revolutionary independence movement, "The Five" were honoured as "Heroes of the Republic of Cuba" and awarded the "Playa Girón" medal.

All of The Five were back in Cuba by then and a new phase had begun. The complete commemoration ceremony was televised. I watched it all. I found it very moving and here are some of the reasons why.

I should say, by way of a preamble, that I guess some less sympathetic to the Revolution will criticise the event and the inclusion of the youth theatre company "La Colmenita" for inculcating the young in revolutionary principles, an element that is often criticised by supporters of the corporate consumer culture and a default response. It is a criticism I might once have expressed. On this occasion, though, I noticed how inspired I was left by the revolutionary principles and appreciation expressed, the creativity, and the respect for all the revolutionary ancestors who gave their lives for the right to sovereignty and self-determination of the Cuban people. The acceptance speech given by Gerardo Hernández, on behalf of the Five, humbly highlighted that they had been rewarded "for having done our duty". He also acknowledged the contribution of Commander in Chief, Fidel Castro, for his stand for "struggle, resistance and sacrifice", reminding us that the word "surrender" has no place in the vocabulary of a revolutionary, proclaiming that they were sharing the award with all Cubans and solidarity groups who have on-goingly supported the revolution, and expressing gratitude and loyalty to the revolutionary Cuba to which they had been able to return, consistent with Fidel Castro's declaration in 2001 in which he stated "Volverán" ("They will return").

In case you are interested, the event was uploaded to Youtube on 25th February 2015 by Cuba Hoy, with the title "*Así conmemoró*

Cuba el 24 de Febrero y homenajeó a los Cinco Héroes" (This is how Cuba commemorated and paid homage to *The Five*). For me, the most poignant part was the young people singing "Blowing in the wind", voicing Bob Dylan's sad reflection of human cruelty and injustice.

How Cubans cope with the hardships of life becomes much more comprehensible when one grasps the philosophical underpinning and the decades of struggle for independence from the former colonisers and imperialists. It really is a case of knowing where you have come from, and the struggle, resistance and sacrifice it has taken, and continues to take, in the face of potential foreign predators.

MOMENT THIRTY-THREE

Buying in hard currency

You might think me pretty daft for not being able to comprehend certain things but I have not yet come to understand how Cubans can buy domestic white goods on standard paltry salaries. Maybe most don't need to as they already have fridges and TVs and washing machines, but if anything breaks or they want to upgrade I guess they have to resort to funds provided by family members living overseas who can send regular remittances.

Of course, any one of the increasing number of room renters receives hard currency on which they clearly pay taxes but they do at least have valuable money coming into the house. This is not the case with the still large numbers of people who work in State jobs and receive their salaries in Cuban pesos.

The smallest refrigerator with a freezer that we found cost $450 and the automatic front-loading washing machine cost $585.

This type of washing-machine is quite a rare commodity in Cuba and one often has to wait until they reappear in the shops after a new international shipment. Deliveries are somewhat irregular and you have to buy when you find what you require as it may disappear. This is true of white goods as well as many other items at certain times. A British friend of mine in Havana had the same experience with apples and wholemeal flour. One day there was no toilet paper in my two nearest shops. The local supply of my preferred Cuban cigarette brand comes and goes.

Neighbours share information about where there is chicken for sale. I always tell my husband when I have managed to find cheese. I tend to look in the Cuban peso shops and I check the hotel shops when I use the internet. I tend to find cheese more regularly. At a price, of course.

MOMENT THIRTY-FOUR

Women, children and home

As far as I can tell, women are honoured and respected as key players in the Revolution and revolutionary intent, and a large number of women work. That said, it seems to me that they are still often expected to take responsibility for a lot of the daily domestic activity such as cooking and cleaning as well. Nature has determined the majority of the child-rearing activity and women's rights around maternity leave from work are sufficiently generous so as to guarantee a still relatively high birth rate, since women have a right to a year's paid leave in Cuba, and a further year without pay. There is, however, no paternity allowance.

The bringing up of children is seen as the woman's role. And if the mother is busy, the resident grandmother will often play her key role. Perhaps because of restricted living accommodation, it is not infrequent to find the grandmother taking on a lot of the role of guide as many families comprising three generations live in the same house.

It seems to me that Cuba is essentially a very matriarchal society, while at the same time demonstrating the traditional *machoism* stereotypically associated very often with Latin countries. The mother in Cuba holds such a revered position that I am reminded of a comment someone made to my father about a similar honour paid to Irish mothers ... An English colleague of my father once said when an Irish fellow was lamenting his mother's absence "What is it about the Irish and their mothers? They seem to think they were the only ones who had them and the rest of us were delivered by stork?"

MOMENT THIRTY-FIVE

Noise

A lot of Cuban houses and flats have slatted windows without glass. There are many advantages to this as the weather conditions can cause major damage if there is a lot of glass around. On top of that, the heat is often oppressive so the ability to partially open windows to allow airflow is an advantage.

In addition, from what I have seen, it is much more difficult to remove the slats if you want to break into someone's house so slats are useful as without them one would have the additional cost of railings over every window.

All of this means that you hear the neighbours' music during most waking hours –and even sleeping ones in some parts of town-, their TV, and even their conversations at times.

Cubans rarely have door bells. If the door is locked or you want to see if someone is home without having to climb stairs, the practical solution is shouting, rather than a quick mobile call which would cost a disproportionate amount. It is not uncommon for fathers or mothers to yell when calling their child in for a shower. It's probably not uncommon in the UK but the number of trees and the distance between houses means that the sound is moderated before reaching inside your own living room. With less than a metre between us and the house next door, a lot of the sounds are overheard.

Of course, when in Old Havana, you will have the almost constant sound of traffic intermingled with the music. Heading down to the Malecón will also provide its own musical accompaniment to the common sound of the sea water breaking over the dogs' teeth rocks.

What you don't find in Havana or the surrounding areas, however, are the constant overhead streams of airplanes or jet engine noise.

MOMENT THIRTY-SIX

Living accommodation

As with many, or perhaps even most things in Cuba, everything is available at a price. Maybe that's true everywhere but Cuba is commonly viewed as dilapidated and decaying, and much of it is, but a tour round parts of Havana like Miramar, where most of the international diplomatic missions are, or even many parts of the municipality of Playa, mostly providing residences for Cubans, can throw up many surprises. There are newly-painted gated properties, many of which house privately-owned cars, and have avocado and mango trees in the backyard. Although I have never seen any from the street, I know some have swimming pools. I have to conclude that these have either all been bought by foreigners resident in Cuba, or with Cuban family members, or by Cubans with money brought back from periods of work overseas.

At the other extreme, there are the *solares* one can still see in Old Havana. These are the tenement buildings, mostly in great need of repair. The majority of these are home to people who have always lived there and would prefer to stay than to move to another part of town where there may be more spacious and more modern accommodation.

In between these two extremes, there is a huge amount of privately-owned accommodation. I was surprised to find that about 80% of it is owned by the people who live in the flats and houses until I discovered the history. Until the 1950s there were a lot of landlords holding many properties and renting them out in the private sector. One of the first revolutionary measures, taking into consideration that much of the property was formerly owned by U.S. landowners, was subject to speculation, and cost an average of a third of household income, was to halve rents which "were among the highest in the world"[6]. In the years following 1959, a review was undertaken and many titles were awarded to the residents who became the owners. The sale of these properties was not allowed until recent changes in the law, although people were able to exchange properties if they found theirs to be either too large or too small for their requirements. Prior to the change in the law a black market had appeared as undeclared money was being exchanged along with the house, hence the change in the law to allow legal sale and purchase.

Foreigners are permitted to buy property only if they have permanent residence in Cuba. I have read a couple of stories on the internet about foreigners who have lost their properties. While I cannot comment on those without knowing specific details, I am aware of someone having lost their property due to them

---

[6] Fidel Castro's address to U.N. September 26, 1960

having undertaken unauthorised building works. My husband told me of a family member who lost the dilapidated but spacious house he lived in with his widowed mother to an unscrupulous carer who managed to persuade the mother to sign the title over to her to ensure everything in her elder care was taken care of. These cases do exist. Sadly you can find unscrupulous people everywhere.

What I have observed is that many people have stayed in the place that became the family home post-1959, either through preference or necessity. Many people who were renting a small apartment or a moderate-sized house back then have since had children and grandchildren resulting in very limited accommodation for ever-increasing families. Maybe as a consequence of the living arrangements and accommodation shortages, or maybe because of the challenge of meeting daily needs and time required for doing what many of us consider simple tasks like shopping, I have not yet met anyone who lives alone, a pretty common occurrence in the UK.

It seems to me like Cubans always have a partner. They may not live with them although they mostly do, despite the evident impact on overall family living in restricted spaces. I am aware also of teenage sons sharing a bed with their siblings, and a mother and grandmother doing the same. As far as I can tell amongst many Cubans cramped living, where even teenage and adult sons share a bed with their widowed or divorced mother, is just one other format. And I also know of those with a spare room and independent bedrooms for the children. You can find everything in Cuba. Disparities and all.

The cramped living arrangements sadden me when I consider how much results from poverty. The upside is the closeness of family and neighbourly relations which allow pots of food to be pulleyed between houses and apartments in hurricane season when the streets can flood and going out is not recommended. While acknowledging the difficulties, to me, this is a very inspiring occurrence which has largely been lost in the singledom of life in what we call the developed world.

The key element here, though, is the level of choice. Shortage of accommodation and funds to rent it, make living with three generations more of a requirement than an option.

MOMENT THIRTY-SEVEN

Sickness in Cuba

I am about to express a very cynical view. Back in the UK I don't recall so many people going on a regular, and almost daily basis, to the doctors' surgery. My cynical view is that, in a country where the medical profession is so famously well-trained, any discomfort is viewed as curable and a visit to the doc is as good a way of spending time as any. It seems though that even the doctors don't show up on occasion but I have no idea if that is because they are treating people in several clinics.

I know many people in the UK who would happily take time off work but back there if you start taking too many days out you are likely to be questioned and you may risk losing your post. Of course, in Cuba, if you don't show up for work employers can sanction by reducing your salary accordingly, although for many who are having to supplement with funds from family members overseas, I would take a guess that the attitude that you might lose 5% of very little is not much of a motivator for turning up day after day. Motivation is understandably lacking as you will not lose your post unless presumably you are working for one of the new entrepreneurs, but employee rights are logically highly defended in the planned Socialist economy.

Days off are one of the things that make it so difficult in Cuba to get some tasks done in a timely fashion as you may well find the people who are dealing with your papers are not available. A personal experience for me was wanting to get an eye test when I realised I probably needed to assist my close-up vision. The specialist was not there to do the eye-test when we turned up and then we were told she was expected back at the end of the week. It occurs to me that the specialist will have her own administrative processes to deal with and will be facing her own delays when she turns up at any other organism to process something. The administrative processes are not yet highly digitalised, making the mounds of paper both difficult to manage and slow to process, maybe unless one can give a little financial motivation.

Interestingly, the new maritime commercial development zones in Mariel and Santiago de Cuba have special conditions which include higher salaries for those employed there. This, it seems, is fundamental to motivating those who are working there to provide the sort of service that will be required by international clients and investors. As ever, medical care will be provided.

MOMENT THIRTY-EIGHT

So is Cuba Socialist or Communist?

There are so many contradictions in economic and business policy in Cuba while the government responds to a changing and challenging world. And so many versions of reports outside Cuba which invoke the highly charged "reds in the bed" Cold War espionage image, that one has to resort to historical and external sources to define the political system in Cuba.

Before we refer to external sources, it is worth noting that the system does not fit easily into any academic description of Socialism or Communism and has been referred to as "Fidelism", a specifically Cuban response to the freedom struggles of the nineteenth century and subsequent subjugation to the U.S., a response embodied in the charismatic persona of Fidel Castro, the historic leader of the Revolution, whose brother now leads the country but who continues to be recognised and acknowledged as the historic leader.

From a brief and very simplistic overview of Cuban history, we learn that the struggle for independence from Spain began alongside independence movements in other Latin American countries, picking up in the 19ᵗʰ century. However, Cuba, with Puerto Rico and the Philippines, were the last Spanish colonies to fall. The U.S. government had an interest in retaining Cuba under its sphere of influence and entered the Cuban War of Independence when it was already advanced. Fidel's 1960 address to the U.N. highlights:

> "The Cubans who had fought for our independence... sincerely believed in the joint resolution of the U.S. Congress of April 20, 1898, which declared that 'Cuba is, and by right, ought to be, free and independent'".

He continues by saying "But that illusion was ended by a cruel deception".

The cruel deception was the declaration which announced U.S. intervention in the independence war against Spain. What then happened is that, far from recognising Cuba's right to be free and independent, the U.S. engaged in a military occupation of the island (given more recent U.S. military and international policies one might assume that this was under the guise of peace-keepers) and established conditions in Cuba's 1901 Constitution, including the establishment of a U.S. military base in Guantánamo and the Platt Amendment which conceded powers to the U.S. government to intervene in Cuba's internal affairs.

In Fidel's 1960 address to the United Nations, he refers to nationalising the electricity, petrol refineries, and other U.S. interests in the early days of the Revolution:

> "We were not 150 per cent communists at that time, we just appeared slightly pink."

The Revolution's early associations with the Soviet Union were a response to the United States' reduction of Cuban sugar imports, justified by Fidel as a simple need to export to other markets. Further collaboration with the former Soviet bloc was born out of need.

That said, while reports of renewed diplomatic relations might include reference to Communism, Raúl's speech on 17th December made reference to Socialism, not once mentioning Communism. It is true that the party of Government in Cuba is called the Communist Party of Cuba, but their policies are aligned with the on-going social revolution. Much of the western media still insist on references to Communist Cuba.

MOMENT THIRTY-NINE

Television in Cuba

One thing that makes me smile in a country where so little happens in a timely fashion is the way they give you the TV scheduling for the evening. It is displayed in text form on the screen but is also read. Being from the UK, I am used to TV programmes starting and ending at hours followed by multiples of five, like 8pm, 8.10 or 8.30. In Cuba they schedule according to the length of the programmes so you find programmes starting at 6.17pm, 8.34, etc. Between programmes there are often public health announcements and, of course, no commercial advertising spots. I have never liked being force-fed a load of fear-mongering insurance company ads or of glitzy products with some spurious benefit allegedly on offer if I buy this product or that, but being reminded to wash my hands does not inspire me either.

Some people do have satellite dishes and most have access to different programmes of the Cuban TV and radio system, as well as TeleSur from Venezuela. Those with satellites can pick up CNN and various U.S. broadcasts, sometimes even those used by the anti-Cuba lobby on occasion to emit subversive content and stimulate discontent, but those issues are not the focus here.

Political speeches are always broadcast on TV and a weekly overview of the news is screened. Many programmes focus on music. You have quiz shows, but obviously without huge prize money as gambling was outlawed with the closure of the large number of Mafia-backed casinos in Havana on the triumph of the Revolution. There are some excellent comedy shows, my favourite being *Pánfilo,* whose content occurs to me as so humorous because it relates to the reality of life in Cuba. His humour exemplifies the lyrics of another of Tony Ávila's songs which contains a line identifying Cubans as the only humans able to laugh so heartily at their own misfortune. There is perhaps an element of "if you don't laugh, you'd end up crying", but the human warmth of Cubans in general is something I have experienced and something which is often commented upon by visitors to the island. They are a people who seem to me to have very little but are always willing to share.

MOMENT FORTY

Are Cubans really friendly or do they just want my money?

When I met my now husband, what some of my friends asked, particularly the Spanish ones who have more experience of Cubans who have migrated to Spain, is "are you sure he's not just using you?"

I admit it is a question I ended up asking myself, particularly when the visa restrictions didn't allow him to work in the UK and I had to support both of us on the money I had saved or was earning. Of course I wondered it because I had been an independent woman for so many years, without a partner, that I, and everyone else around me, believed that I was going to spend the rest of my life alone as a single woman. They were used to me being alone and I hadn't spent my life lamenting the absence of a man in my life.

So it was obvious why friends and other people were asking that question. I understand it. What I didn't much like was the refusal of most of them to recognise that they themselves were prejudiced. Some of them spoke as if they had absolute knowledge about every Cuban who had ever married a foreigner. Or maybe they were concerned because I, like them, wasn't expecting me to get married at this stage in my life.

So, back to the question... Are they really friendly? In my experience, I have to say "yes". They are a people who have a life expectancy equal to that of developed countries, and they have an enjoyment of life which is reflected in their personal relationships. They spend time with family and make time to get together with friends and neighbours, which are very important in Cuba.

There are many problems to deal with and many are solved by sharing with neighbours who will tell you where certain products have become available. Or they will lend you something you need on a short-term basis, or maybe simply spend some time discussing problems they have managed to resolve.

Cubans seem to like foreign visitors. Maybe it is because it allows them to recognise that they and their country have something to offer and the people who come have not been deterred from visiting despite all the negative media reports. An opportunity to share their revolutionary success and to inform and enlighten. And at least they have the sort of climate that the grey skies of the former Soviet bloc – the other demonised Communist regimes - did not enjoy, and many of the beaches and *cayos* of Cuba, this pearl of the Caribbean, are acknowledged for their natural beauty. Many Cubans I have met celebrate their good fortune in this regard.

For sure, the money you leave in the country will be welcome but in my experience many people are friendly and interested in talking to foreigners to be able to share experiences, and learn about life outside Cuba.

There is a legally defined offence on the statute books which specifically relates to harassing tourists. Some tourists, aware of the practice of *jineterismo,* seem to arrive with the intention of finding a stunning *mulata.* I see examples of these older foreign men who can spend a comparatively small amount of money on the almost constant company of a local girl who will show them round the delights of the city day and night. It is possible that many of the young women can celebrate the income but I have seen many who look uncomfortable with their role and their often old, ugly and fat companion. Sadly it is a feature of the areas with the greatest concentration of tourists, and while I do not condone it, I do have some understanding and compassion for many of the girls who see this form of activity as their best option for providing for their families. It is widely acknowledged that it is just one further form of income generation in a country with huge internal disparities and clear evidence of international economic imbalances.

Prostitution is a subject that has been dealt with in Cuban cinema also, highlighting the motivations and the risks, one of which is that anyone found offering this sort of service risks a prison sentence of a minimum of two years, and this is imposed.

Quite separately, one aspect of the Cuban attitude to foreigners which strikes me every time I hear it, and I have heard it quite a bit, is that Cubans distinguish between the people of the United States and the government of the United States. They recognise the U.S. and Cuba share many of the same roots and cultural heritage and Cubans widely acknowledge that it is the U.S. government which has imposed the sanctions and which has the responsibility now to resume respectful relationships between the two countries. On account of this, every Cuban I have heard mention the increasing numbers of North American tourists in Havana in the beginning of 2016 did so with satisfaction knowing that they now have the opportunity to show U.S. citizens what Cuba is really like and what it has to offer.

MOMENT FORTY-ONE

The Weather

You'll have to excuse me for being so banal as to include a section on the weather but I cannot resist sharing this as yet another of the (to me) surprising aspects of this country.

I have been in Cuba most frequently in the month of February. On my first visit, I spent my time at the Havana International Book Fair slowly roasting. During my most recent February visit in 2015, I was wearing a t-shirt, a blouse, a jumper and later in the afternoon, as the rain threatened, I had to put on the overcoat that my husband had put in the rucksack, more aware of how cold it can be up in the old Spanish Cabaña fortress. It's cold, not because of low temperatures, but mostly because of the wind.

What now seems most common in Havana in February is the cold fronts coming from the north. The rain in May can go on most of the day, and while the temperatures remain relatively high, the sky can be a constant grey. The month of August tends to be characterised by heavy rain showers which you can almost set your watch by. I have not been in Havana in any hurricane season. An avid experience-seeker, I admit that I am not on a mission to have that experience.

One fact that the Cuban people are proud of is that, despite severe weather conditions at times, their preventative and rescue services are very efficient and as a result the hurricanes have claimed fewer lives than in natural disasters in many other countries.

If you plan to travel to the island in May or June, make sure you pack the mosquito repellent. Not expecting flies can ruin a trip. Personally I take repellent whatever time of year I go because you can never know. I have been stung on every visit probably on account of always wanting to spend time by water. But those mozzies do get everywhere and you won't always find repellent easily. So I take some.

MOMENT FORTY-TWO

Workmanship

I have seen a lot of evidence of shoddy workmanship. Clearly a lot of work has to be done with whatever materials they can get hold of at a price they can afford. As a result, a lot of Cubans do their own repairs and building jobs, calling on experienced friends, or friends of friends, wherever possible. It seems that unless a workman comes with various recommendations from trusted sources, it's best to do maintenance yourself.

The other thing to bear in mind is that the minute they see a foreigner in the house, you can pretty much guarantee the price will go up. So here again my husband is in charge of all negotiations.

MOMENT FORTY-THREE

Health services in Cuba

You probably already know that Cuban medics have participated in many international humanitarian missions. In Sierra Leone, dealing with the Ebola crisis, there have been more medical staff from Cuba alone than from *Médecins sans Frontières* and the World Health Organisation together.

The Cuban Government provides medically qualified personnel to Venezuela to staff clinics in the poorest areas. The conditions are not always favourable. Many of the clinics in Venezuela have been attacked by anti-Government protesters. Venezuelans have been able to receive medical treatment in Cuba under bilateral agreements, in much the same way that Maduro's predecessor, Hugo Chávez Frías, did when dealing with his eventual terminal cancer. Some might think that the fact Hugo Chávez eventually died is not a great recommendation for the Cuban health service but then we would probably have to ask medical specialists about the nature of his disease and consider whether doctors can *always* save a life, or if the human condition involves physical death.

Visitors from many countries have come to take part in so-called "health tourism" in Cuba, triggering the Government to introduce in the last few years a requirement to have medical insurance on entering the country. I guess it's a recognition of the value of Cuban health care and for which they may as well earn income in hard currency, like any other service offered to tourists.

The health services are wide-ranging and there are many services that would be classed in the UK or Spain as preventative and alternative, while in Cuba a more holistic approach tends to be adopted. Treatment is not limited to pharmaceutical solutions or surgery, although of course these are applied where appropriate.

It is not uncommon for Cubans who have been living abroad to return home to be treated by their own national health service if faced with a serious illness. What is to me remarkable is that surgery appears to be a last resort rather than an early stage solution, and treatment in many hospitals in Cuba refers patients to practitioners of what we would call "alternative therapies" including acupuncture, massage, Reiki, QiQong, Tai Chi and yoga, all services offered for free, alongside all medical services under the public health service.

My own experience with the health service has, happily, been limited. Three years ago in our area there was a widely-publicised case of cholera which coincided with my stomach responding to a change in diet or something, causing me to manifest some symptoms similar to those of cholera. As it turned out, I was not suffering from the disease but I did learn that if there is a suspected outbreak of a disease, there is no requirement for health care insurance before being treated, foreigner or not. I also experienced a remarkable level of attention with home visits over three days from a doctor, two nurses and two medical students from Venezuela, until they were sure that I was not suffering any further symptoms. I can't say I was impressed with the state of the one hospital clinic I went into, but I was certainly left with the experience of really being cared for.

Unsurprisingly, health services for the people are a fundamental right incorporated into the Revolution's commitment.

MOMENT FORTY-FOUR

Endnote

When I set myself the target of completing this volume by the end of February, capturing a moment in time, I did not expect further negotiations to be taking place on the penultimate day of the month.

We are at the beginning of a process which currently has no end date. Even fifteen months down the line, President Obama has not yet put the lifting of the blockade to Congressional vote, perhaps for fear of the outcome not being favourable. The Cuban government has made clear their stand that the United States' continuing economic and financial blockade against their country is contradictory to the spirit of tolerance and respect, and therefore inconsistent with renewed diplomacy. They have also made clear that they intend to continue to support humanitarian causes around the world.

There will undoubtedly be many aspects of life in Cuba I have not touched, many elements which historians understand, and principles by which Cubans live and which make their hardships easier to tolerate, which I have omitted. This is a short volume. An introduction to a new phase. It is not intended to be comprehensive nor exhaustive. I trust, however, it has provided some insights which will assist you in understanding the current state of the country and the lives of Cubans.

I was in Cuba a year after the announcement of renewed diplomatic relations. I expect to be able to tell you more about what is changing very soon.

APPENDICES

APPENDIX I

Extracts of address by President Raúl Castro
Downloaded from Granma.cu 7 November 2015 at http://
en.granma.cu/cuba/2014-12-17/statement-by-the-cuban-president
Published December 17, 2014 12:12:51

Fellow countrymen ... willingness to hold a respectful dialogue ...
on the basis of sovereign equality ... without detriment to the
national independence and self-determination of our people.

... willingness to discuss and solve our differences without
renouncing any of our principles.

The heroic Cuban people ... faithful to our ideals of independence
and social justice.

Strongly united ...
... deepest gratitude
... agreed to renew diplomatic relations.

APPENDIX II

Some extracts of the Statement by the President on Cuba Policy Changes

https://www.whitehouse.gov/the-press-office/2014/12/17/statement-president-cuba-policy-changes (downloaded 7 November 2015) and a slightly different version downloaded on March 17, 2016 found at https://www.whitehouse.gov/the-press-office/2014/12/17/statement-president-cuba-policy-changes

Cabinet Room

12:01 P.M. EST

THE PRESIDENT: Good afternoon. Today, the United States of America is changing its relationship with the people of Cuba.

In the most significant changes in our policy in more than fifty years, we will end an outdated approach that, for decades, has failed to advance our interests, and instead we will begin to normalize relations between our two countries. Through these changes, we intend to create more opportunities for the American and Cuban people, and begin a new chapter among the nations of the Americas...

… America's steadfast opposition to communism.
… an ideological and economic barrier hardened between our two countries.

Meanwhile, the Cuban exile community in the United States made enormous contributions to our country –- in politics and business, culture and sports. Like immigrants before, Cubans helped remake America, even as they felt a painful yearning for the land and families they left behind. All of this bound America and Cuba in a unique relationship, at once family and foe.

APPENDIX III

Message from the Five Heroes

The following text was published in the Granma newspaper on 12 September 2013 http://www.granma.cu/idiomas/miami5/ingles/683.html

This is how it begins

• **To the conscience of the world and the U.S. people:**

FIFTEEN years ago today, September 12, 1998, the brutality of five simultaneous arrests burst into our homes to initiate one of the most shameful chapters of U.S. legal history: the trial of those of us today known as The Five.

The arrest and trial of The Five will remain in history as one of the most ignominious and vile episodes of relations between the United States and Cuba.

APPENDIX IV

Will the U.S. finally condemn its own blockade of Cuba?

Author: Jackie Cannon, published October 9, 2015 in The Canary

downloaded from http://www.thecanary.co/2015/10/09/will-us-finally-condemn-blockade-cuba/ (9 Nov 2015)

Presidents Castro and Obama: Summit of the Americas (April 2015)

Despite the renewal of diplomatic relations between Cuba and the U.S., announced in December 2014, and the subsequent removal of Cuba from the U.S. list of countries designated as State Sponsors of Terrorism, the blockade remains in place.

An upcoming vote at the UN, condemning the continuing U.S. sanctions against Cuba, will provide further indication of whether there is real interest in making life better for Cubans, or if this is just a different way of presenting imposed regime change on the sovereign Republic of Cuba and its people.

If you look west, away from the crises happening to our east and the human suffering which is being caused in the name of democracy and regime change, it seems that there is considerable excitement about the new era of diplomatic relations between Cuba and the United States, after over 50 years of impasse, hostility and critically, blockade and sanctions.

Look a bit deeper and you start to see that the first steps towards 'normalisation' have been taken: embassies opened in each of the countries, the U.S. easing its sanctions on its citizens travelling to the island, Pope Francis flying direct to Washington from Cuba, and President Raúl Castro attending the United Nations General Assembly in New York in September 2015.

But they are baby steps. Some trade agreements have already been negotiated, notably in potential joint research into the Cimavax lung cancer vaccine. What is not, however, being highlighted is that 'normalised' relations are not possible while the U.S. maintains its blockade of its neighbour.

The upcoming UN vote is worth watching out for. There is an opportunity for the Obama administration to vote with most of their allies and join the international call to end the blockade. Senator Marco Rubio, a voice of the anti-Cuba lobby industry, suggests that the U.S. president would be 'putting international popularity ahead of the national security and foreign policy interests of the United States.' Maybe it's time to focus on how out of line the U.S. blockade of Cuba is in terms of international platforms. The last 23 years have seen up to 188 votes in favour of ending the blockade at the UN, with just two 'no' votes coming from the U.S. and Israel, with 3 outlying groups of Pacific islands abstaining.

It might be a bit much to expect Obama's administration to vote to end the blockade, thereby contradicting the U.S.' own laws and coming head-to-head with Congress. An abstention from the U.S., albeit rather absurd, would likely be more acceptable to anti-Cuba lobbyists than an expressed vote against maintaining the blockade. However, if the U.S. really care about making life better for Cubans, decisive action to end the blockade with a congressional vote is the only outcome that is really going to make a difference. That would overcome one normalisation hurdle. Although the stand-off continues over Guantánamo, the return of which is being demanded by Cuba, but which the U.S. has said is not up for negotiation.

APPENDIX V

Israel's UN vote dilemma over U.S. blockade of Cuba

Author: Jackie Cannon, published October 20, 2015 in The Canary

U.S. Secretary of State John Kerry, currently visiting Europe, is scheduled to meet with Mahmoud Abbas and Benjamin Netanyahu this week to discuss an end to escalating tensions between Israel and Palestine. But with just a week to go before the 24th UN vote on ending the U.S. blockade against Cuba, due on 27 October, is there a chance that Netanyahu and Kerry will discuss their intentions regarding the vote in the light of renewed diplomatic relations between the U.S. and Cuba?

Right now, reports of their planned meeting are understandably focusing on a solution for Israeli / Palestinian relations, and on the gulf between Obama and Netanyahu in their dealings with Iran. The issue of the blockade against Cuba may not be at the top of the agenda but it remains to be clarified.

For the last 23 years, the U.S. and Israel have been the only two countries to repeatedly vote in the UN in favour of maintaining the U.S. blockade against Cuba. Rumours are abounding that the U.S. is considering abstaining from the vote. Whatever the U.S. decides to do, the situation is odd for Israel, a country that has supported the U.S. in return for staunch support of its own international policies.

Obama's administration and Benjamin Netanyahu have not always agreed on issues. In July of this year, John Kerry referred to Netanyahu's reaction to a deal between the U.S. and Iran as "way over the top", adding the Israeli Prime Minister didn't even know what the concessions were that "the U.S. had not engaged in".

It would be no surprise to learn that Israel had no idea of what concessions had been afforded to Cuba, heightening suspicions, given these tensions were reported six days before the reopening of the Cuban Embassy in Washington.

According to The Times Of Israel:

Israel was caught totally off-guard by the American about-face when the U.S. and Cuba announced diplomatic relations being resumed in December 2014. The article continued:

> For years, Jerusalem had unquestioningly followed
> Washington's lead on Cuba, considering it routine
> and necessary backing given America's unstinting
> support for Israel in various international forums.
> Then America made its sudden, drastic shift

toward Cuba. But Israel cannot follow suit —
not at the moment, anyway — because Havana
isn't interested in ties with Israel before going on
to highlight "Cuba's vicious Israel-bashing".

There is no evidence for allegations of "Israel-bashing" unless you want to label Cuba's support for the Palestinians' humanitarian plight as that. Cuban internationalist policy since 1959 has participated in solidarity missions across the planet. Supporting the Palestinian people is not "Israel-bashing". In the same way as the Cuban government and ordinary Cubans often express their condemnation of the U.S. government while having no issue with the North American people, Cuba has been critical of Israeli government policy without any bashing of the people.

Crucially, as outlined in this succinct <u>review</u> of Israel-Cuba relations,

Havana has never challenged Israel's right to exist.

Indeed, the historic leader of the Revolution, Fidel Castro, a key figure even since the Presidency passed to his brother, Raúl, expressed in a 2010 <u>interview</u> his sympathy with persecuted Jews throughout history, a gesture which was received with an expression of gratitude from the Israeli Prime Minister. President Shimon Peres wrote to Fidel Castro <u>describing his comments</u> as:

a surprising bridge between the hard reality and
a new horizon.

This expression of appreciation was <u>not welcomed</u> by the staunchly anti-Cuban Republican congresswoman, Ileana Ros-Lehtinen, who urged Netanyahu to retract his acknowledgement of the former Cuban President. As the incoming chairwoman of the House Committee on Foreign Affairs, committed to ousting Cuba's Revolutionary government, she opposed a diplomatic opening between Cuba and Israel, closed since 1973.

Cuba had unexpectedly broken diplomatic ties with Israel at that time as Fidel Castro allegedly sought to lead the Non-Aligned Movement, news which Israel reportedly received with surprise and <u>regret</u>. Certainly one could argue that in the context of non-aligned nations not attached to following the policy of a super-power, breaking diplomatic relations with any country that voted unquestioningly with the U.S. could appear to be a logical step.

Forty years on and the context has shifted between Cuba and the U.S. Outdated hostilities are up for review. The pressure in the U.S. to lift the blockade is mounting from <u>both sides</u> of the political spectrum. Many U.S. businesses are unwilling to lose out further on potential trade opportunities with the neighbouring island. However, until the blockade is lifted, and Guantánamo is returned to Cuba, all steps taken since December 2014 remain tentative and reversible. This makes the UN vote critical.

All in all it is an absurd situation, leaving Israel to determine whether to abstain (or consider abstaining), vote alongside their U.S. allies in the bewildering event that the U.S. votes against its own laws, or become the only country to vote to maintain the blockade against a country with which they appear to have no particular beef.

Whether, or whichever way, Israel votes, is likely to be decided according to the message they want to communicate to the U.S. rather than any particular axe to grind with Cuba.

APPENDIX VI

Why is the U.S. still blockading Cuba?

Author: Jackie Cannon, published October 29, 2015 in The Canary

downloaded from http://www.thecanary.co/2015/10/29/us-still-blockading-cuba/ (9 Nov 2015)

At the end of last year it looked hopeful that Cuba was finally going to be able to benefit from the new-found spirit of engagement with the U.S. Despite some progress, the stalemate continues and Cuban people are still suffering.

On Tuesday we witnessed the presentation, for the 24th time, of Cuba's draft resolution to the United Nations General Assembly: "Necessity of ending the economic, commercial and financial embargo imposed by the United States of America against Cuba." Despite the renewal in December 2014 of diplomatic relations between Cuba and the U.S., for the 24th time the U.S. and Israel again stood alone by voting against lifting the blockade.

Last year, there were three abstentions in the UN vote. This year, for the first time ever, there were none. Aside from the two "no" votes, the resolution was supported unanimously, with the remaining 191 nations voting in favour of Cuba's draft resolution.

Many people listened to President Obama's <u>political rhetoric</u> in December 2014 of "normalization", with his encouraging opening line:

> Today, the United States of America is changing
> its relationship with the people of Cuba.

to which he added:

> no other nation joins us in imposing these
> sanctions.

Although he does not mention the continued support from Israel, the fact that, for the first time ever, no country abstained in Tuesday's vote, is an even clearer confirmation of no other nations joining the U.S. in the sanctions.

Many U.S. politicians, such as Jeb Bush and Marco Rubio, have <u>denounced</u> Obama's keenness to adopt a new approach towards Cuba. And, of course, it is of note that the focus was on the "relationship with the people of Cuba", not the government.

In December, Obama further declared:

I also believe that more resources should be able
to reach the Cuban people.

That might have indicated an end to sanctions, a precondition
to normalisation required by the Cuban government. There was
reason to hope that this year the U.S. administration would act in
accordance with the spirit of engagement expressed by Presidents
Castro and Obama ten months ago. U.S. Secretary of State John
Kerry, various Congressmen and women, and Senators have all
visited Cuba this year. They were apparently universally satisfied
that their own designation of Cuba as a state sponsor of terrorism
was not appropriate. The designation was removed in May after
no case was presented for it remaining in place.

Progress has been achieved in relations between the two countries.
However, in the draft resolution presented to yesterday's United
Nations General Assembly, Cuba's Foreign Minister, Bruno
Rodríguez Parrilla, highlighted the ongoing enforcement by
the U.S. of the 1996 Helms-Burton Act. The Act embeds the
blockade, in place since 1960, in law by imposing penalties on
third countries trading with Cuba in an express attempt to force a
change of government in Cuba, thereby interfering with national
sovereignty and Cuba's right to self-determination.

Rodríguez Parrilla made a clear call to President Obama to exercise
his presidential powers to curb the application of the economic,
commercial and financial blockade with the words:

> While it is up to the U.S. Congress to adopt
> the decision to put an end to the blockade, the
> President has broad executive prerogatives to
> substantially modify its practical implementation
> and its humanitarian and economic impact.

Conveying a key element of <u>Cuba's message</u>, Rodriguez Parrilla continued:

> Historically, the United States has intended to establish its domination and hegemony on our homeland and, since 1959, it has tried to change the political, economic and social system that our people, fully exercising the right to self-determination, has freely chosen. Some spokespersons from the U.S. Government have declared that the announced Cuba policy is about a change of methods, not goals. Should this be the case, the process towards the normalization of relations between the United States and Cuba will face very serious obstacles.

> The lifting of the blockade will be the essential element that will give some meaning to the progress achieved in the last few months in the relations between both countries and shall set the pace towards normalization.

As has been recognized by President Barack Obama, the lifting of the blockade serves the U.S. national interest and is the will its citizens.

We find that the rumours reported last week in <u>The Canary</u> relating to Israel's stance and a possible abstention by the U.S. in the unenforceable UN resolution vote depended on Cuba rewording the resolution. The U.S. administration was <u>holding out for a revision</u> to Cuba's draft resolution claiming it did "not 'fully reflect' the new spirit of engagement between the former cold war foes".

Nor does a continuing economic, commercial and financial blockade. Rodríguez Parrilla's address to the UN points to sanctions applied since December which also fail to reflect this new spirit of engagement.

The Cuban government remains clear and insistent. The blockade has to end before normalisation can result. Raúl Castro stated this in December 2014:

> Cuba reiterates its willingness to cooperate in multilateral bodies, such as the United Nations. While acknowledging our profound differences, particularly on issues related to national sovereignty, democracy, human rights and foreign policy, I reaffirm our willingness to dialogue on all these issues. I call upon the Government of the United States to remove the obstacles hindering or restricting ties between peoples, families, and citizens of both countries, particularly restrictions on travelling, direct post services, and telecommunications.

Rodríguez Parrilla reiterated the same in Tuesday's resolution:

> But the measures adopted by the U.S. Administration, which came into force on January 16 this year and were later on expanded on September 18, although positive, only modify, in a very limited way, some elements related to the implementation of the blockade.

And that is not the whole picture. In Rodriguez Parrilla's words:

> Any attempt to condition the lifting or modification of the blockade to the introduction of internal changes in Cuba will be in no way acceptable nor productive.

While acknowledging "progress achieved in the course of last year", it is clear that <u>President Raul Castro's words</u> from December 2014 still pertain:

> I have reiterated in [sic] many occasions our willingness to hold a respectful dialogue with the United States on the basis of sovereign equality, in order to deal reciprocally with a wide variety of topics without detriment to the national independence and self-determination of our people.

So the stalemate continues. Cuba continues to demand its right to equality and self-determination and call for the end of what the U.S. calls the "embargo". Meanwhile the U.S. continues to apply sanctions while no vote on their removal is presented to the Republican-majority U.S. Congress, the only body with competence to change the law.

We can celebrate that the way has been opened for normalisation but we cannot ignore that, so far, all advances to date remain tentative. With no change in the law, the blockade can be applied with the same vigour as it has been to date. One could speculate that this allows U.S. companies to implant themselves in Cuba while applying sanctions to other countries wishing to take advantage of the new engagement with the U.S. That may be simple cynicism.

It may be true that with U.S. presidential elections due next year, and Obama not permitted to stand for a third term, the U.S. "no" vote may have more to do with their own internal politics. The fact remains that for now any statements about making life better for Cubans are more easily understood as the language of rhetoric, not reality. For now it looks like all those people who have been rushing to Cuba "before it changes" have a bit more time. The people in Cuba, meanwhile, are obliged to suffer the harsh consequences.

APPENDIX VII

2015 Key Dates

17 December 2014: Presidents Raúl Castro and Barack Obama announce renewal of diplomatic relations

15 January 2015: President Obama announces the lifting of a number of travel restrictions for U.S. citizens, increasing the range of legitimate purposes deemed acceptable for visits to the island.

29 May 2015: Rescission of Cuba as a State Sponsor of Terrorism

1 July 2015: Obama announces re-opening of embassies in Havana and Washington
https://www.whitehouse.gov/the-press-office/2015/07/01/statement-president-re-establishment-diplomatic-relations-cuba

20 July 2015: Cuba opens Embassy in Washington

14 August 2015: U.S. Embassy opens in Havana

19-22 September 2015: Pope Francis visits Cuba on his way to Pastoral trip to the U.S.

5 October 2015: The Cuban Five are honoured by President Evo Morales of Bolivia as heroes of Latin America

27 October 2015: U.S. and Israel vote for 23rd time against lifting blockade on Cuba

APPENDIX VIII

Additional suggested reading:

I would recommend pretty much anything written by A. Kapcia, including "Cuba in Revolution: A History since the Fifties", and articles such as this in *Open Democracy* (6 November 2015) https://opendemocracy.net/antoni-kapcia/end-of-cuban-revolution. Keith Bolender also makes sense to me. You might also find Richard Gott's "Cuba: A New History" valuable.

"To Speak the Truth: Why Washington's 'Cold War' against Cuba Doesn't End", Fidel Castro & Che Guevara (edited by Mary-Alice Waters, Pathfinder Press, 1992), is a very interesting read of the leaders' speeches.

I enjoyed "Cuba: The Land of Miracles – A journey through modern Cuba", by Stephen Smith, although it is was written in 2005.

It is always worth keeping an eye on *Granma International* *(granma.cu)* to see what is being reported on the island. Enjoy seeing if it is the same as in your local press.

Printed in the United States
By Bookmasters